In the middle of the night...

FLORENCE M. TAYLOR
tells you why she wrote FROM EVER-LASTING TO EVERLASTING

This book I wrote for anyone interested in exploring the Bible to see what God is saying in it to those who are living in these troubled times; and also for anyone who would like to enrich his personal language of prayer by a study of Bible prayer passages.

About a year and a half ago, I was drawn into the fellowship of a new church which caught my interest because it seemed to me to be re-creating in our present day an experience very similar to that of the first century Christians in the Book of Acts. And I found myself studying the Bible with a new sense of excitement and joy.

I had retired a number of years ago, and had reached the point where I had no intention of writing any more books. But one night in the wee, small hours, I was suddenly wide awake, and the plan for this book was there in my mind, full-blown.

I have always felt that whatever ability I had in writing was a gift from God to be used only under his guidance. But this time the guidance was clearer and more specific than ever before. I started writing the book the next day, and the Bible study involved became a source of great enrichment, deepened understanding, and a vivid awareness of the presence of God.

I pray that God will similarly bless everyone who picks up the book.

FROM EVERLASTING TO EVERLASTING

Lord, thou hast been our dwelling-place in all generations. Before the mountains were brought forth, or ever thou hadst formed the earth and the world, even from everlasting to everlasting, thou art God.   —Psalm 90:1–2

From Everlasting to Everlasting

Promises and Prayers
Selected from the Bible

FLORENCE M. TAYLOR

The Seabury Press New York

Contents

To the Reader

This collection of Biblical promises and prayers has grown out of the conviction that one way of appropriating for ourselves these mined nuggets of Biblical truth and inspiration is to personalize them—listening to God's promises in his Word as though they were addressed directly to us (which, of course, they are!) and responding directly and personally to him in words sanctified over centuries of use by countless dedicated, Spirit-filled individuals.

In order to increase for us today this personal meaning in both the promises and the prayers, the original text has often been slightly altered. Some of the promises, for instance, have been changed from the third person (i.e., "The Lord will—") to the first person ("I, thy God, will—"). And in a similar way many prayerful meditations *about* God (i.e., "The Lord is my shepherd") have been altered to direct discourse ("Thou art my shepherd, Lord").

It will be clear from this that the Bible references following the selections do *not* always indicate exact quotations, but rather the passage in which the basic idea occurs.

This book has been designed primarily as a book of personal devotions. It is hoped that its use will encourage the reader to commit to memory many of the Biblical treasures included. For generations the value of "learning by heart" (What a lovely phrase!) favorite Scripture passages has been recognized as one way of enriching the spiritual life.

When reminders and affirmations of God's reality, of his sufficiency for every need, of his invincible power, saturate the mind and heart, these thoughts form a persistent undergirding just below the consciousness, ready to be drawn up into the conscious mind as need arises. This is one way in which the deep desires of the heart for holy living can be constantly reinforced and nourished.

When affirmations of this kind are set to music, they tend to be even more haunting and unforgettable. The Bible is a singing book. Its total message is one of redemptive good news for all people that finds appropriate expression in joyous song; and the spirit of praise and thanksgiving is everywhere present in its pages.

Two booklets with many singable melodies of this kind are:

Psalter (Dedicated to the singing of Scriptures in the congregation). Bethany Missionary Association, 612 Dawson Ave., Long Beach, California 90814 ($1.00).

Renewal in Song, compiled by Carol Perkins. Logos International, 185 North Ave., Plainfield, New Jersey 07060 ($1.75).

Try out for yourself the value of learning these selections and singing songs of this kind at frequent intervals throughout the day. This is an effective way of enriching your prayer life while your hands are busy with routine tasks. You may also find value and joy in creating similar melodies for other Biblical selections that speak to your heart.

The beneficial effect of having the subconscious mind

crowded to overflowing with positive, Spirit-filled thoughts and melodies can hardly be overestimated. In moments of unconcentrated mental drifting, the mixed contents of the subconscious bubble up into the conscious. On a mundane level, have you not occasionally been annoyed by the persistent cropping up into your mind of some innocuous TV singing commercial? How much better if the bombardment from the subconscious can be a steady barrage of the eternal Biblical verities that feed the soul!

As I have been working on the book, I have been continuously aware of the debt I owe to a host of dearly loved friends, ministers, and other fellow-members of the universal church of Christ, with whom I have shared rich experiences of worship and Bible study through the years. Though they are not named, their influence is on every page.

This book is offered with the sincere prayer that it may be a means of spiritual enrichment to every reader, as it has already been to the compiler.

F.M.T.

Columbus, Ohio

Part I

SELECTED
BIBLICAL
PROMISES

I am the Lord thy God: hearken
unto my voice.

—Deuteronomy 28:2

About the Promises

Peter's second general epistle has something to say about God's promises. It begins:

Simon Peter, a servant and an apostle of Jesus Christ, to them that have obtained like precious faith with us through the righteousness of God and our Saviour, Jesus Christ,

Grace and peace be multiplied unto you through the knowledge of God and of Jesus Christ our Lord . . .

Whereby are given unto us exceeding great and precious promises that by these we might be partakers of the divine nature having escaped the corruption that is in the world.

—2 Peter 1:1–4

The exceeding great and precious promises, both in the Old and the New Testaments, are given to us for a purpose: that by them "we might be partakers of the divine nature." Christians in many times and places through the centuries bear witness to these truths:

that the rich gifts God has promised us, his people, are instantly and eternally available—all we have to do is to claim them in faith; and

that our appropriation of these divine resources of God's providing, absolutely insures the triumphant and glorious fulfillment of his purpose for us: that we become "partakers of the divine nature."

LIMITATIONS ON THE PROMISES

1. The promises of God are freely given but they cannot be received without an active response on our part. In the prophecy of Obadiah to the "house of Jacob" these words occur:

But upon Mount Zion shall be deliverance, and there shall be holiness, and the house of Jacob shall possess their possessions.
—Obadiah 17 *

At first glance there seems to be a contradiction here. Are not "possessions" by definition things already possessed? Why then is it necessary to "possess" them? Further consideration, however, discloses the interesting fact that there is actually a difference between legal possession and experiential possession.

Take the illustration of a bequest that has been made to you in someone's will. The items listed in the will are legally yours as soon as the will is probated. It is possible, however, for a considerable space of time to elapse between the time of legal possession and the time when you claim and take over the bequests. Occasionally bequests may lie unclaimed for years.

A similar situation often exists in the realm of our spiritual life. The word "testament" also means "will." In God's Word, in his "Will," he has made to each one of us, his children, countless bequests. These are in the form of faithful promises: the things promised have already been given to us. They are ours. We are entitled to them. They are our possessions. It only remains for us to take possession of them —to make them ours in actual experience.

* I am indebted to the Rev. Willard J. Jarvis, pastor of The Redeemer's Church, Columbus, Ohio, for bringing this verse to my attention, and also for much of the interpretation of it included in this section.

2. In claiming these possessions an attitude of confident expectation is necessary. Unless we believe in God, and in his faithfulness to fulfill his promises, there is little likelihood of our successfully "possessing" them.

We need to pray for faith like that of Abraham, of whom it is written:

. . . who against hope believed in hope, and being not weak in faith, staggered not at the promise of God through unbelief, but was strong in faith, giving glory to God; being fully persuaded that, what he had promised, he was able to perform.

—Romans 4:18–21

3. The promises of God are ours only if our hearts are right with him. Do you remember when Simon the sorcerer came to Peter? He said:

Give me also this power, that on whomsoever I lay my hands, he may receive the Holy Ghost.

But Peter said to him, Thy money perish with thee, because thou hast thought that the gift of God may be purchased with money.

Thou hast neither part nor lot in this matter for thy heart is not right with God. —Acts 8:19–21

What does it mean for our hearts "to be right with God"? Page through the Scriptures searching out the promises of God, and notice how frequently these take the form of "If you—, then I—."

To mention just a few:

If ye will obey my voice and keep my covenant, then ye shall be unto me an holy nation. —Exodus 19:5–6

If ye walk in my statutes, I will walk among you.

—Leviticus 26:3,12

When thou art in tribulation if thou turn to me and be obedient to my voice, I will not forsake thee.

—Deuteronomy 4:30–31

I will rejoice over thee for good, if thou turn unto me with
all thy heart.   —Deuteronomy 30:9–10

Just as an act of appropriation and an attitude of confident expectation are necessary if we are to possess our possessions, so also is it necessary for us to "turn unto God with
all our hearts," yielding willing obedience as our part of the
covenant relationship. (It should be noted that promised
gifts are not conditional upon our good works—they are
not earned. They are free gifts as soon as our hearts are
"right with God.")

4. The promises of God are for spiritual growth and
power—"that we might become partakers of the divine
nature." They are not insurance against the trials and
tribulations which are a part of every life. What they are
is the relevation of unlimited and available resources to
meet every spiritual need—to provide the ability to live triumphantly in the face of the worst that life can do to us.

IN CONCLUSION

How changed our lives would be if we were to appropriate the glory and the power freely available to us! What
joy, and peace, and hope, and courage are ours for the tak-
ing. And what blessed fruit we might produce in the lives
of others if we would completely surrender our lives to God,
enabling him to use us to witness powerfully for him, to
serve sacrificially, to love redemptively.

Old Testament Promises

I have spoken by my prophets. —Hosea 12:10

Many of the promises of God, spoken "in times past unto the fathers by the prophets," were limited promises in the sense that they had to do with specific events in a specific time and situation.

One whole group of promises, those referring to the coming of God's Son, Jesus, as the Messiah, has not been included because they have already been fulfilled.

The promises gathered here have universal and eternal significance. Their relevance for us today, and for the needs and problems of our times, is as great as it was in the days when they were spoken. Never has it been more important than it is today to listen to this word and similar words from God's Book:

Be strong and of a good courage; be not afraid, neither be thou dismayed, for I, the Lord thy God, am with thee whithersoever thou goest.   —Joshua 1:9

Glory in the Lord

The Lord God is a sun and shield;
the Lord will give grace and glory;
no good thing will he withhold
from them that walk uprightly.
            —Psalm 84:11

I Will Uphold Him

Trust in me, the Lord, and do good.
Delight thyself in me
    and I will give thee
    the desires of thine heart.
Commit thy way unto me,
    trust also in me,
    and I shall bring forth
    thy righteousness as the light.
The steps of a good man
    are ordered by me,
    and I delight in his way.
Though he fall he shall not
    be utterly cast down;

for I will uphold him
with my hand.
                    —Psalm 37:3–6,23–24

If—Then

Now therefore,
  if ye will obey my voice indeed,
  and keep my covenant,
  then ye shall be
  a peculiar treasure unto me
  above all people:
  for all the earth is mine:
And ye shall be unto me
  a kingdom of priests
  and an holy nation.
                    —Exodus 19:5–6

In Tribulation

When thou art in tribulation
  if thou turn to me, thy God,
  and shalt be obedient
  unto my voice,
  (for I, the Lord thy God,
  am a merciful God)
  I will not forsake thee.
                    —Deuteronomy 4:30–31

I Will Rejoice Over Thee

I, the Lord thy God,
    will make thee plenteous
    in every work of thine hand,
    in the fruit of thy body,
    and in the fruit of thy land:
I will rejoice over thee for good,
    if thou shalt hearken unto my voice,
    to keep my commandments,
    and if thou turn unto me, thy God,
    with all thine heart,
    and with all thy soul.
For this commandment which I command thee,
    it is not hidden from thee,
    neither is it far off.
    It is not in heaven,
    that thou shouldest say,
    Who shall go up for us to heaven
    and bring it unto us
    that we may hear it, and do it?
    Neither is it beyond the sea,
    that thou shouldest say,
    Who shall go over the sea for us,
    and bring it to us,
    that we may hear it and do it?
    But the word is very nigh thee,
    in thy heart,
    that thou mayest do it.
            —Deuteronomy 30:9–14

As Mount Zion

They that trust in me, the Lord,
　　shall be as Mount Zion,
　　which cannot be removed,
　　but abideth forever.
As the mountains are
　　round about Jerusalem,
　　so I, the Lord,
　　am round about my people,
　　from henceforth, even forever.
　　　　　　—Psalm 125:1–2

I Shall Bless Thee

I, the Lord,
　　shall greatly bless thee,
　　only if thou carefully
　　hearken unto my voice,
　　to do all the commandments
　　which I command thee.
For I, the Lord thy God,
　　will bless thee
　　as I promised thee.
　　　　　　—Deuteronomy 15:4–6

Reap in Joy

The Lord hath done great things for us;
　　whereof we are glad.

They that sow in tears shall reap in joy.
He that goeth forth and weepeth,
    bearing precious seed,
    shall doubtless come again
    with rejoicing,
    bringing his sheaves with him.
        —Psalm 126:3,5–6

I Have Called Thee by Thy Name

Fear not, for I have redeemed thee,
    I have called thee by thy name;
    thou art mine.
When thou passest through the waters,
    I shall be with thee,
    and through the rivers,
    they shall not overflow thee:
    when thou walkest through the fire,
    thou shalt not be burned;
    neither shall the flame kindle
    upon thee.
For I am the Lord thy God,
    thy Saviour,
    fear not: for I am with thee.
        —Isaiah 43:1–5

Like the Palm Tree

The righteous shall flourish
    like the palm tree;
    he shall grow
    like a cedar in Lebanon.

Those that be planted
　　in the house of the Lord
　　shall flourish
　　in the courts of our God.
　　They shall bring forth fruit
　　in old age.
　　　　　　　—Psalm 92:12–14

Fear Not, Neither Be Dismayed

Be strong and of a good courage:
　　I, the Lord, will go before thee;
　　I will be with thee,
　　I will not fail thee,
　　neither forsake thee:
　　fear not, neither be dismayed.
　　　　　　　—Deuteronomy 31:6,8

Unto the Hills

Lift up thine eyes unto the hills;
　　from whence cometh thy help.
　　Thy help cometh from me, the Lord,
　　who made heaven and earth.
I shall not suffer thy foot to be moved;
I, who keep thee, shall not slumber.
Behold, I shall neither
　　slumber nor sleep.
I, the Lord, am thy keeper.
I am thy shade upon thy right hand.
The sun shall not smite thee by day,
　　nor the moon by night.

I shall preserve thee from all evil.
I shall preserve thy soul.
I shall preserve thy going out
    and thy coming in
    from this time forth,
    and even for evermore.
               —Psalm 121

My Chosen Fast

Is not this the fast that I have chosen?
    to loose the bands of wickedness,
    to undo the heavy burdens,
    and to let the oppressed go free,
    and that ye break every yoke?
Is it not
    to deal thy bread to the hungry?
    when thou seest the naked
    that thou cover him?
Then shall thy light break forth
    as the morning, and thine health
    shall spring forth speedily;
    and thy righteousness
    shall go before thee;
Thou shalt call, and I will answer;
    thou shalt cry, and I shall say,
    Here am I.
Then shall thy light rise in obscurity,
    and the darkness be as the noon day;
    and I, thy God,
    shall guide thee continually,
    and satisfy thy soul.
            —Isaiah 58:6–11

I Will Walk Among You

If ye walk in my statutes,
   and keep my commandments
   and do them,
   then I will give you rain
   in due season,
   and the land shall yield
   her increase,
   and the trees of the field
   shall yield their fruit.
And I will have respect unto you,
   and make you fruitful,
   and establish my covenant
   with you.
And I will walk among you,
   and will be your God;
   and ye shall be my people.
          —Leviticus 26:3–4,9,12

My Word Shall Prosper

My thoughts are not your thoughts,
   neither are your ways my ways.
   For as the heavens
   are higher than the earth,
   so are my ways
   higher than your ways,
   and my thoughts than your thoughts.
For as the rain cometh down

and the snow from heaven,
and returneth not thither,
but watereth the earth
and maketh it bring forth and bud,
that it may give seed to the sower,
and bread to the eater,
so shall my word be
that goeth forth out of my mouth;
it shall not return to me void,
but it shall accomplish
that which I please,
and it shall prosper
in the thing whereto I sent it.
  —Isaiah 55:8–11

An Everlasting Covenant

Incline your ear, and come unto me,
 hear, and your soul shall live,
 and I will make
 an everlasting covenant with you;
 for I, the Holy One, have glorified thee.
  —Isaiah 55:3,5

They Shall All Know Me

Behold, the days come, saith the Lord,
 that I will make a new covenant
 with my people:
 I will put my law
 in their inward parts,

and write it in their hearts;
and will be their God,
and they shall be my people.
And they shall teach no more
every man his neighbor,
and every man his brother,
saying, Know the Lord:
for they shall all know me,
from the least of them
unto the greatest of them.
— Jeremiah 31:31–34

Great and Mighty Things

Call unto me, the Lord thy God,
and I will answer thee,
and show thee great and mighty things,
which thou knowest not.
And I will reveal unto thee
the abundance of peace and truth.
— Jeremiah 33:3,6

Swords Into Plowshares

In the last days it shall come to pass
that the mountain of my house
shall be established
in the top of the mountains,
and it shall be exalted above the hills;
and people shall flow unto it.
And many nations shall come and say,
Come, let us go up

to the mountain of the Lord,
and to the house of God;
and he will teach us of his ways,
and we will walk in his paths:
for the law shall go forth of Zion,
and my word from Jerusalem.
And I will judge among many people,
and rebuke strong nations afar off;
and they shall beat their swords
into plowshares,
and their spears into pruning-hooks:
nation shall not lift up a sword
against nation,
neither shall they learn war any more.
But they shall sit every man
under his vine and under his fig tree;
and none shall make them afraid:
for I, the Lord of hosts,
have spoken it.
            —Micah 4:1–4

The Covenant of My Peace

I, the Lord, thy Redeemer,
will have mercy on thee
with everlasting kindness;
For the mountains shall depart,
and the hills be removed,
but my kindness
shall not depart from thee,
neither shall the covenant
of my peace be removed.
            —Isaiah 54:8,10

I Will Pour Out My Spirit

And it shall come to pass afterward,
    that I will pour out my spirit
    upon all flesh; and your sons
    and your daughters shall prophesy,
    your old men shall dream dreams,
    your young men shall see visions.
And whosoever shall call upon my name
    shall be delivered.
                    —Joel 2:28,32

The Blossoming Desert

The wilderness, and the solitary place
    shall be glad,
    and the desert shall rejoice,
    and blossom as a rose,
    it shall blossom abundantly
    and rejoice with joy and singing.
Strengthen ye the weak hands
    and confirm the feeble knees;
    ye that are of a fearful heart,
    be strong, fear not;
    behold, I, your God,
    will come and save you.
Then the eyes of the blind
    shall be opened,
    and the ears of the deaf
    shall be unstopped.
    Then shall the lame man

leap as an hart,
and the tongue of the dumb
shall sing;
for in the wilderness
shall waters break out,
and streams in the desert.
And the parched ground
shall become a pool,
and the thirsty land,
springs of water.
And my ransomed people shall come
with songs of everlasting joy;
they shall obtain joy and gladness,
and sorrow and sighing
shall flee away.
　　　　　—Isaiah 35

I Will Be Found of You

I, the Lord, know the thoughts
that I think toward you,
thoughts of peace,
and not of evil.
And ye shall call upon me,
and ye shall go and pray unto me,
and I will hearken unto you.
And ye shall seek me,
and find me,
when ye shall search for me
with all your heart.
And I will be found of you.
　　　　　—Jeremiah 29:11–14

Walk in My Ways

And what do I, the Lord your God,
   require of you, my people,
   but to walk in all my ways,
   and to love me,
   and to serve me,
   with all your heart,
   and with all your soul,
   to keep my statutes,
   which I command you
   for your good?
          —Deuteronomy 10:12–13

New Testament Promises

I have spoken by my Son. —Hebrews 1:2

The whole New Testament is, in essence, one glorious promise of God "spoken to us by his Son." This promise is summed up in what is probably the most quoted single verse in the whole Bible:

For God so loved the world, that he gave his only begotten Son, that whosoever believeth in him should not perish, but have everlasting life.   —John 3:16

To select from the rich promises scattered through the New Testament those to include in the present volume has been a difficult but delightful task. Obviously, the final selection represents the favorite passages of the compiler! Inevitably, many people will look for their favorite promises and not find them. This may not, however, prove a total loss. This book is not designed to take the place of the Bible itself; rather it seeks to stimulate the reader's interest in the Word, and to send him back to it with renewed appetite to discover more of its treasures and new values in old, familiar passages.

O taste and see that the Lord is good.   —Psalm 34:8

Seek First the Kingdom

Take no thought for your life,
   what ye shall eat,
   or what ye shall drink;
   nor yet for your body,
   what ye shall put on.
Is not the life more than meat,
   and the body than raiment?
For your heavenly Father
   knoweth that ye have need
   of all these things.
But seek ye first
   the kingdom of God
   and his righteousness;
   and all these things
   shall be added unto you.
          —Matthew 6:25,32–33

Ask—Seek—Knock

Jesus said:
   Ask and it shall be given you,
   seek and ye shall find;
   knock and it shall
   be opened unto you.
          —Matthew 7:7

The House on the Rock

Whosoever heareth these sayings of mine,
    and doeth them,
    I will liken him unto a wise man
    who built his house upon a rock:
    And the rain descended,
    and the floods came,
    and the winds blew
    and beat upon that house
    and it fell not,
    for it was founded upon a rock.
                —Matthew 7:24–25

Two or Three

Jesus said:
    Again I say unto you,
    that if two of you shall agree
    on earth as touching anything
    that they shall ask,
    it shall be done for them
    of my Father which is in heaven.
    For where two or three
    are gathered together in my name,
    there am I in the midst of them.
                —Matthew 18:19–20

Whatsoever Ye Shall Ask

Verily, verily, I say unto you,
   he that believeth on me,
   the works that I do,
   shall he do also,
   and greater works than these
   shall he do;
   because I go unto my Father.
   And whatsoever ye shall ask
   in my name, that will I do,
   that the Father may be glorified
   in the Son.
   If ye shall ask anything
   in my name, I will do it.
           —John 14:12–14

Believe

What things soever ye desire,
   when ye pray,
   believe that ye receive them,
   and ye shall have them.
           —Mark 11:24

Inasmuch

When the Son of man shall come
   in his glory,
   then shall the King say
   unto those on his right hand,

Come, ye blessed of my Father,
inherit the kingdom prepared for you
from the foundation of the world:
for I was an hungered and ye gave me meat;
I was thirsty, and ye gave me drink.
I was a stranger, and ye took me in;
naked, and ye clothed me;
I was sick, and ye visited me;
I was in prison, and ye came unto me.
Verily I say unto you,
inasmuch as ye have done it
unto one of the least of these,
my brethren, ye have done it
unto me.
And these righteous shall go away
into life eternal.
           —Matthew 25:31,34–46

My Word

Verily, verily, I say unto you,
he that heareth my word,
and believeth on him that sent me,
hath everlasting life
and is passed from death
into life.
           —John 5:24

Gift of the Holy Spirit

If a son shall ask bread
    of any of you that is a father,
    will he give him a stone?
    Or if he ask a fish,
    will he for a fish
    give him a serpent?
    Or if he shall ask an egg,
    will he offer him a scorpion?
If ye then, being evil,
    know how to give good gifts
    to your children,
    how much more
    shall your heavenly Father
    give the Holy Spirit
    to them that ask him?
                —Luke 11:11–13

Manifold Gifts

Verily, I say unto you,
    there is no man
    that hath left house, or parents,
    or brethren, or wife, or children,
    for the kingdom of God's sake,
    who shall not receive
    manifold more in this present time,
    and in the world to come
    life everlasting.
                —Luke 18:29–30

The Water of Life

> Behold, my tabernacle is with men,
>> and I will dwell with them,
>> and they shall be my people,
>> and I myself will be with them,
>> and be their God.
> And I will wipe away
>> all tears from their eyes;
>> and there shall be no more death,
>> neither sorrow, nor crying,
>> neither shall there be any more pain;
>> for the former things are passed away.
> Behold, I make all things new.
>> I am the Alpha and Omega,
>> the beginning and the end.
> I will give unto him that is athirst
>> of the fountain
>> of the water of life freely.
>> He that overcometh
>> shall inherit all things;
>> and I will be his God,
>> and he shall be my son.
>>> —Revelation 21:3–7

The Freeing Truth

> If ye continue in my word,
>> then are ye my disciples indeed;
>> and ye shall know the truth,
>> and the truth shall make you free.
>>> —John 8:31–32

Many Mansions

In my Father's house
    are many mansions;
    if it were not so,
    I would have told you.
    I go to prepare a place for you,
    and if I go
    and prepare a place for you,
    I will come again
    and receive you unto myself;
    that where I am
    there ye may be also.
                —John 14:2–3

Unto the End of the World

All power is given unto me,
    in heaven and in earth.
Go ye, therefore,
    and teach all nations,
    baptizing them
    in the name of the Father,
    and of the Son,
    and of the Holy Ghost,
    teaching them to observe
    all things whatsoever
    I have commanded you;
    and lo, I am with you alway,
    even unto the end of the world.
                —Matthew 28:18–20

Bread of Life

I am the bread of life;
　　he that cometh to me
　　shall never hunger.
I am the living bread
　　which came down from heaven;
　　if any man eat of this bread,
　　he shall live forever.
　　　　　　　　—John 6:35,51

The Spirit of Truth

If ye love me
　　keep my commandments.
And I will pray the Father
　　and he shall give you
　　another Comforter,
　　that he may abide with you forever,
　　even the Spirit of truth,
　　whom the world cannot receive
　　because it seeth him not,
　　neither knoweth him,
　　but ye know him
　　for he dwelleth with you
　　and shall be in you.
　　　　　　　　—John 14:15–17

Joy

Verily, verily, I say unto you,
   that ye shall weep and lament,
   but the world shall rejoice;
   and ye shall be sorrowful,
   but your sorrow
   shall be turned into joy.
Ye now therefore have sorrow,
   but I will see you again,
   and your heart shall rejoice,
   and your joy
   no man taketh from you.
           —John 16:20,22

The Promise Is Unto You

Repent, and be baptized,
   every one of you,
   in the name of Jesus Christ
   for the remission of sins,
   and ye shall receive
   the gift of the Holy Ghost.
For the promise
   is unto you
   and to your children,
   and to all that are afar off,
   even so many
   as the Lord our God shall call.
           —Acts 2:38–39

Ask and Receive

Ask, and ye shall receive,
    that your joy may be full.
                —John 16:24

My Peace I Give Unto You

Peace I leave with you,
    my peace I give unto you;
    not as the world giveth,
    give I unto you,
Let not your heart be troubled,
    neither let it be afraid.
                —John 14:27

The Peace of God

In everything by prayer
    and supplication
    with thanksgiving
    let your requests
    be made known unto God.
And the peace of God
    which passeth all understanding
    shall keep your hearts and minds
    through Jesus Christ.
                —Philippians 4:6–7

The Light of Life

I am the light of the world;
  he that followeth me
  shall not walk in darkness
  but shall have
  the light of life.
          —John 8:12

I Will Draw Nigh

God hath said:
  Draw nigh to me,
  and I will draw nigh to you.
          —James 4:8

The True Vine

Jesus said:
  I am the true vine,
  and my Father is the husbandman.
  Abide in me, and I in you,
  As the branch cannot bear fruit
  of itself,
  except it abide in the vine,
  no more can ye,
  except ye abide in me.
  I am the vine, ye are the branches.

He that abideth in me, and I in him,
the same bringeth forth much fruit;
for without me ye can do nothing.
           —John 15:1,4–5

The Closed Door

Behold, I stand at the door
    and knock:
    if any man hear my voice,
    and open the door,
    I will come in to him,
    and will sup with him,
    and he with me.
                —Revelation 3:20

God's Sufficiency

God is able
    to make all grace
    abound toward you;
    that ye, always having
    all sufficiency in all things,
    may abound to every good work;
    being enriched in everything
    to all bountifulness,
    which causes through us
    thanksgiving to God.
                —II Corinthians 9:8,11

A Crown of Life

Be thou faithful unto death
and I will give you
a crown of life.
—Revelation 2:10

Good Cheer

These things have I spoken unto you
that in me ye might have peace.
In the world ye have tribulation,
but be of good cheer;
I have overcome the world.
—John 16:33

Come, Lord Jesus

Jesus said:
Surely I come quickly. Amen.
Even so, come, Lord Jesus. Amen.
—Revelation 22:20

Part II

SELECTED BIBLICAL PRAYERS

I am the Lord thy God: I
will hear you.
        —Zechariah 10:6

About Prayer
and Biblical Prayers

> When thou saidst to me, Seek ye my face, my heart said
> unto thee, Thy face, Lord, will I seek.   —Psalm 27:8

All prayer is in response to God's prior activity. If it were
not for his creative love brooding over his creatures, no
"upward reach" would stir within our hearts.

DOES GOD ANSWER PRAYER?

Prayer makes no sense at all unless the pray-er has within
his heart the deep conviction of the reality of a personal
God. Christians define this reality as "the God and Father
of our Lord Jesus Christ."

Many people today, while professing "belief in God,"
and claiming the name of Christians, yet tend to limit
God's activity in their own minds to times long past and
(perhaps) to times in the far future. The moment the
claim is made that God is operative *now*, *today*, in ways
beyond our understanding, these nominal Christians are
apt to be uncomfortable, and to circumscribe God's activity
by some such explanatory phrases as, "The age of miracles

is past," or "God works through natural law." Even healing miracles are sometimes explained away by claiming that as scientific knowledge increases, some "reasonable" explanation of them will be found.

To the question, "Do you believe in prayer?" people with these points of view, if they are completely honest, would be forced to answer, "No," or to give some qualified affirmative to the effect that "prayer may have a positive value in that it may change the attitude of the pray-er."

The lack of positive, affirmative belief in prayer as the means of channeling into human lives the power of almighty God, is undoubtedly the reason why prayer today has become for many people a mere formality, lacking all vitality and effectiveness.

Believing Christians, on the other hand, respond to the question, "Does God answer prayer?" with an unequivocal and positive "Yes!" They contend that God hears and answers, in his own way and time, every sincere prayer that burdened human hearts breathe out.

Incontrovertible evidence exists, and continues steadily to accumulate, that God does today perform miracles in response to prayer, just as he did in the early days of Christianity. His power is no less in modern times than it ever was.

David Wilkerson's *The Cross and the Switchblade** is one contemporary account of God's repeated action in response to prayer requests. *Like a Mighty Wind* by Mel Tari** is another record of modern-day miracles. This reads like a sequel to the story of the early Christian church as recorded in the book of Acts—which is precisely what it is.

* A Spire Book, published by Pyramid Publications for the Fleming H. Revell Company, by arrangement with Bernard Geis Associates, 1964.
** As told to Cliff Dudley. Published by Creation House, Inc. 433 East St. Charles Rd., P.O. Box 316, Carol Stream, Illinois, 60187. 1971.

Thoughtful persons who honestly investigate these and similar strange phenomena find it difficult to dismiss the accumulating evidence as "coincidence," or "hysteria," or "illusion." The least that can be said is that here is a mystery, a deep and awe-inspiring mystery, to be accepted with reverent wonder and humility.

Frequently the person propounding the question "Does God answer prayer?" is actually asking a different question.

WILL GOD GRANT ME THAT FOR WHICH I PRAY?

To this question the most ardent believer in answered prayer must in all honesty reply: "Not always." Frequently, yes, but definitely not always. The Bible teaching on this point is clear and inescapable. Consider two instances.

Paul testifies:

And lest I should be exalted above measure through the abundance of the revelations, there was given to me a thorn in the flesh.

For this thing I besought the Lord thrice, that it might depart from me.   —II Corinthians 12:7–8

Paul's "thorn in the flesh" was not removed. And if further evidence were needed of God's not granting some specific requests, Jesus' prayer in Gethsemane comes vividly to mind:

Father, if thou be willing, remove this cup from me: nevertheless not my will, but thine, be done.   —Luke 22:42

In spite of his prayer, Jesus drained the bitter cup to the dregs.

The believing Christian, presenting his requests to God, prays with full knowledge and complete acceptance of the possibility that his request may be denied. This does not weaken his conviction that God is actively directing his life. Though he cannot always understand why a specific request is denied, he trusts that God has a reason for withholding his desire, and that in due time the reason will become evident.

Experience seems to prove that God *always* grants sincere prayers for spiritual resources: for stronger faith, for strength to withstand temptation, for power to endure without bitterness trials and sufferings, for courage, for wisdom, for guidance, for increased compassion and love. Never do we pray sincerely for these things without an infilling of the Spirit to meet the need for which we pray. For prayers of this kind, the promise, "Whatever ye ask in prayer, believing, ye shall receive" (Matthew 21:22), is unfailingly fulfilled.

When a specific request is not granted, we need to reaffirm our belief in God as "the loving Father of our Lord Jesus Christ." This belief carries with it the unalterable faith that God, our Holy Father, craves for each of his children the highest and best possible experience. We hold fast to the belief that all things that come to us in life (both the seeming good and the seeming evil) are from God's hand, and that whatever he gives us (or denies) is for our ultimate, highest good. Even though he may send the exact opposite of that for which we pray, it is only our limited understanding that causes us to see it as evil.

Three questions that Jesus once asked his followers have a bearing on this point:

What man is there of you, whom if his son ask bread, will he give him a stone?

Or if he ask a fish, will he give him a serpent?

If ye, then, being evil, know how to give good gifts unto your children, how much more shall your Father which is in heaven give good things to them that ask him?   —Matthew 7:9–11

In this passage, perhaps, lies part of the answer to the "why" of God's granting some requests and denying others. Even loving human fathers are wise enough not to grant all the requests of their children. They refuse to give them those things which may endanger their lives; they withhold those things which may prove harmful; they insist often on unpleasant things that are necessary for the child's well-being. In our human experience it often seems to be the *unloving, indifferent* parent who gives in to his child's every whim.

God's gifts are always for our highest good. When in his infinite wisdom he knows our prayer is for something harmful, something that would prove a stumbling block to our finest maturing, he withholds it. He refuses to give us "a stone," even when we ask for it, when what we really need is "bread."

Think once again of Jesus' prayer in Gethsemane. Surely his death on the cross must have seemed to those who loved him, unmitigated tragedy and evil. Looking back across the centuries, however, it is clear, that if he had escaped the cross, the whole purpose of his life would have been thwarted. It was necessary for him to make the final and complete surrender in order that God might use him as his instrument for the salvation of mankind.

GUIDELINES FOR PERSONAL PETITIONS

What guidance can we find for ourselves and our petitions in all this somewhat bewildering evidence? Surely no one is bold enough to claim any final answers in this whole area of communication between God and his creatures. The best we can hope to do is to recognize some tentative guidelines:

—As God's children we have the privilege of making known to him the desires of our hearts.
—We ask in faith, firmly believing in God's limitless power and that he always wills whatever is for our ultimate good.
—We ask in Jesus' name. Only those things that are in accord with his spirit and teachings are legitimate requests.
—We pray with thanksgiving, gratefully acknowledging the blessings we have received, the Lordship of Jesus in our lives, and our complete dependence on our Father.
—We believe that a prayer request is "unanswered" or denied, *not* because God is unable or unwilling to give us our heart's desire, but because in his infinite wisdom and tender love, he knows that the granting of this particular prayer would interfere with his divine purpose for our highest good.

THE FAITH TOWARD WHICH WE GROPE

The faith which we seek in our prayer life is more than mere acceptance of the inevitable. It is implicit trust in God: the conviction that his will for us, his guidance of every aspect and experience of our lives, is always for our highest good, even when every "reasonable" indication seems to point in the opposite direction.

The faith toward which we grope is the conviction that the most difficult and unwelcome experiences, accepted *with thanksgiving* as directly from God's hand, will be used by him to forward his ultimate and totally beneficent purpose for our lives.

THE LORD'S PRAYER

Any consideration of Biblical prayers would be incomplete without mention of the Lord's Prayer. In A *Series of Sermons on the Lord's Prayer,* Dr. Morgan Noyes had this to say:

The one thing which his disciples asked Jesus to teach them was the art of prayer. They came to him saying, "Lord, teach us to pray." He gave them a form of words which we call "The Lord's Prayer." . . .

There is always a danger in using forms of words in prayer. We become so familiar with the words that we rattle them off without stopping to remember what they mean. That is what has happened to the Lord's Prayer. Words can be nothing but meaningless sounds. But they can also be ladders for the spirit. So Jesus gave his disciples a model prayer, and taught them *that when they put themselves into his words, his words could become their prayer, linking them in spirit with the living God.*

OTHER SCRIPTURAL PRAYERS

While of course the Lord's Prayer is the outstanding prayer in the Bible, no Christian can afford to miss the enrichment of his prayer life which comes through appropriating for his own the prayer resources scattered all through the Scriptures.

Here again, as in the promises, many prayers have necessarily been omitted in this limited collection. Every reader will want to add to those given here special passages which speak directly to his need.

Of Praise and Adoration

> Holy, holy, holy art thou, O Lord of hosts: the whole
> earth is full of thy glory.   —Isaiah 6:3

The Isaiah story begins:

> In the year that king Uzziah died I saw the Lord sitting upon a
> throne, high and lifted up, and his train filled the temple. Above
> it stood the seraphim; and one cried unto another, and said,
> Holy, holy, holy is the Lord of hosts: the whole earth is full of
> his glory.   —Isaiah 6:1–3

In studying and searching through the Bible for prayers
for this book, I was surprised that so many of the prayers
and prayerful passages proved to be expressions of praise
and adoration. And as I pondered this, it came to me that
this may be a neglected area in the prayer life of many of
us today.

Is it possible that we think of prayer chiefly as petition,
sometimes for ourselves, sometimes for others? Are we
driven to prayer in times of crisis? Or when we are burdened
with guilt for wrong-doing? And do many of us perhaps
neglect the all-important steady focussing of our hearts and
minds on the illimitable greatness and goodness and power
and love of God, and on his instant and continuous avail-
ability? If all our periods of personal and group prayer were

to begin with an attempt to focus on God's reality and abiding presence, surely the content of the prayers that followed would be transformed and irradiated by faith, and hope and love.

Bless Us, O Lord

Bless us, O Lord, and keep us.
Make thy face shine upon us,
    and be gracious unto us:
    lift up thy countenance upon us
    and give us peace.
                —Numbers 6:24–26

The Greatness of God

Thou art great, O God,
Thou art the Rock.
Thy work is perfect
    for all thy ways are judgment.
A God of truth, and without iniquity,
    just and right art thou.
                —Deuteronomy 32:3–4

As an Eagle

As an eagle stirreth up her nest,
    fluttereth over her young,

spreadeth abroad her wings,
taketh them,
beareth them on her wings,
So thou, Lord, dost lead us.
                    —Deuteronomy 32:11

O Most High God

O most high God,
    how great are thy signs!
    How mighty are thy wonders!
Thy kingdom is
    an everlasting kingdom,
    and thy dominion is
    from generation to generation.
                    —Daniel 4:2–3

Thine Is the Greatness

Thine, O Lord, is the greatness,
    and the power, and the glory,
    and the victory, and the majesty;
    for all that is in the heaven
    and in the earth is thine;
Thine is the kingdom, O Lord,
    and thou art exalted
    as head above all.
Both riches and honour
    come of thee, O Lord,
    and thou reignest over all;
    in thy hand is power and might;

and in thine hand
it is to make great,
and to give strength unto all.
Now therefore our God, we thank thee
and praise thy glorious name.
—I Chronicles 29:11–13

Strangers and Sojourners

We are strangers and sojourners
before thee, O God,
as were all our fathers;
our days on the earth
are as a shadow
and there is none abiding.
O Lord our God,
keep this forever
in the imagination
of our thoughts,
and prepare our hearts unto thee.
—I Chronicles 29:15,18

Hannah's Prayer

My heart rejoiceth in thee, O Lord.
There is none so holy as thou,
for there is none beside thee,
neither is there any rock
like thee, O God.
Thou, Lord, art a God of knowledge,
and by thee are actions weighed.

Thou, Lord, makest poor,
    and makest rich;
        thou bringest low, and liftest up.
Thou wilt keep the feet of thy saints,
    and the wicked shall be silent
    in darkness.
                —I Samuel 2:1–9

Blessed Be Thy Glorious Name

We bless thee, O Lord our God,
    for ever and ever.
Blessed be thy glorious name
    which is exalted
    above all blessing and praise.
Thou, even thou, art Lord alone;
    thou hast made heaven,
    the heaven of heavens,
    with all their host,
    the earth, and all things
    that are therein,
    the seas, and all that is therein,
    and thou preservest them all;
    and the host of heaven
    worshippeth thee.
Thou art the Lord our God.
                —Nehemiah 9:5–7

A Refuge for the Oppressed

Thou, Lord, wilt be a refuge
    for the oppressed,
    a refuge in time of trouble.
And they that know thy name
    will put their trust in thee;
    for thou, Lord, hast not forsaken
    them that seek thee.
        —Psalm 9:9–10

The Earth Is Thine

The earth is thine, O Lord,
    and the fulness thereof,
    the world,
    and we who dwell therein.
        —Psalm 24:1

How Excellent Is Thy Name

O Lord our Lord,
    how excellent is thy name
    in all the earth!
    who hast set thy glory
    above the heavens.
When I consider thy heavens,
    the work of thy fingers,
    the moon and stars

which thou hast ordained;
what is man
that thou art mindful of him?
and the son of man
that thou visitest him?
For thou hast made him
a little lower than the angels,
and hast crowned him
with glory and honour.
Thou madest him to have dominion
over the works of thy hands;
thou hast put all things
under his feet;
all sheep and oxen, yea,
and the beasts of the field,
the fowl of the air,
and the fish of the sea,
and whatsoever passeth
through the paths of the seas.
O Lord, our Lord,
how excellent is thy name
in all the earth!
　　　　　—Psalm 8

The Heavens Declare

The heavens declare thy glory, O God,
and the firmament showeth
thy handiwork.
Day unto day uttereth speech,
and night unto night
showeth knowledge.

There is no speech nor language
    where their voice is not heard.
    Their line is gone out
    through all the earth,
    and their words
    to the end of the world.
              —Psalm 19:1–4

The Fountain of Life

In the fear of thee, O Lord,
    is strong confidence;
    and thy children shall have
    a place of refuge.
The fear of thee, O Lord,
    is a fountain of life,
    to depart from the snares of death.
              —Proverbs 14:26–27

Under Thy Wings

Thy mercy, O Lord, is in the heavens,
    and thy faithfulness
    reacheth unto the clouds.
Thy righteousness is like
    the great mountains;
    thy judgments are a great deep;
O Lord, thou preservest man and beast.
How excellent
    is thy lovingkindness, O Lord!
    therefore the children of men

put their trust
    under the shadow of thy wings;
    for with thee is the fountain of life;
    in thy light shall we see light.
O continue thy lovingkindness
    unto them that know thee
    and thy righteousness
    to the upright in heart.
                —Psalm 36:5–10

My Light and My Salvation

Thou, Lord, art my light
    and my salvation;
    whom shall I fear?
Thou, Lord, art the strength
    of my life;
    of whom shall I be afraid?
One thing have I desired of thee,
    O God, that will I seek after:
    that I may dwell in thy house
    all the days of my life.
                —Psalm 27:1,4

My King of Old

Thou, God, art my King of old,
    working salvation
    in the midst of the earth.
Thou didst divide the sea
    by thy strength;

thou didst cleave
the fountain and the flood:
thou driedst up mighty rivers.
The day is thine,
the night also is thine;
thou hast prepared the light
and the sun.
Thou hast set all the borders
of the earth;
thou hast made summer and winter.
—Psalm 74:12–17

All Nations Shall Come

All nations whom thou hast made
shall come and worship
before thee, O Lord,
and shall glorify thy name.
For thou art great
and doest wondrous things;
thou art God alone.
Teach me thy way, O Lord;
I will walk in thy truth.
I will praise thee, O Lord God,
with all my heart.
I will glorify thy name
forever more.
Thou, O Lord, art a God
full of compassion,
and gracious, longsuffering
and plenteous in mercy
and truth.
—Psalm 86:9–12,15

Thy Glorious Name

Blessed be thou, Lord God,
  who only doest
  wondrous things.
And blessed be thy glorious name
  for ever.
And let the whole earth
  be filled with thy glory;
  Amen and Amen.
      —Psalm 72:18–19

Unto Thee Be Glory

Now unto thee, O God,
  the King eternal,
  immortal, invisible,
  the spirit of wisdom,
  be honour and glory
  for ever and ever. Amen.
      —I Timothy 1:17

Thou, O Lord, Reignest

Thou, O Lord, reignest,
  thou art clothed with majesty;
  thou art clothed with strength,
  wherewith thou hast girded thyself;
  the world also is stablished
  that it cannot be moved.

Thy throne is established of old;
    thou art from everlasting.
    The floods have lifted up, O Lord,
    the floods have lifted up
    their waves.
Thou, Lord on high, art mightier
    than the noise of many waters,
    yea, than the mighty waves
    of the sea.
            —Psalm 93:1–4

Excellent Things

Thou, O God, art my salvation;
    I will trust and not be afraid:
    for thou, O Lord,
    art my strength and my song.
I will sing unto thee, O Lord,
    for thou hast done
    excellent things:
    this is known in all the earth.
            —Isaiah 12:2,5

Who Can Be Compared Unto Thee?

The heavens shall praise
    thy wonders, O Lord,
    for who can be compared unto thee?
Thou rulest the raging of the sea:
    when the waves thereof arise
    thou stillest them.
The heavens are thine,

the earth also is thine:
as for the world
and the fulness thereof,
thou hast founded them.
The north and the south,
thou hast created them.
Justice and judgment are
the habitation of thy throne:
mercy and truth
shall go before thy face.
Blessed be thou, O Lord,
for evermore.
Amen and Amen.
—Psalm 89 (selected verses)

A *Shadow from the Heat*

O Lord, thou art my God;
I will exalt thee,
I will praise thy name;
for thou hast done
wonderful things;
thy counsels of old
are faithfulness and truth.
For thou hast been
a strength to the poor,
a strength to the needy
in his distress,
a refuge from the storm,
a shadow from the heat.
Lo, thou art our God;
we have waited for thee,
and thou wilt save us;

thou art our God;
we have waited for thee,
we will be glad and rejoice
in thy salvation.
                    —Isaiah 25:1–4,9

The Knowledge of Thy Glory

Thou, O God, who commanded the light
    to shine out of darkness,
    hast shined in our hearts
    to give the light
    of the knowledge of thy glory
    in the face of Jesus Christ.
                    —II Corinthians 4:6

Who Else But Thee?

Who else but thee, O God,
    hath measured the waters
    in the hollow of his hand,
    and meted out heaven with the span,
    and comprehended the dust
    of the earth in a measure,
    and weighed the mountains in scales,
    and the hills in a balance?
With whom didst thou take counsel,
    and who instructed thee,
    and taught thee knowledge
    and showed to thee
    the way of understanding?
                    —Isaiah 40:12,14

Omnipresence

Whither shall I go from thy spirit?
　　or whither shall I flee
　　from thy presence?
If I ascend up into heaven,
　　thou art there;
　　if I make my bed in hell,
　　behold, thou art there.
If I take the wings of the morning
　　and dwell in the uttermost parts
　　of the sea,
　　even there shall thy hand lead me,
　　and thy right hand shall hold me.
If I say,
　　Surely the darkness shall cover me,
　　even the night shall be
　　light about me. Yea, the darkness
　　hideth not from thee;
　　but the night shineth as the day;
　　the darkness and the light
　　are both alike to thee.
　　　　　　　—Psalm 139:7–12

None Like Thee

There is none like unto thee, O God;
　　thou art great,
　　and thy name is great in might.
Who would not fear thee,

O King of nations?
forasmuch as among
all the wise men of the nations,
and in all their kingdoms,
there is none like unto thee.
Thou, Lord, art the true God,
and an everlasting king.
Thou hast made the earth
by thy power,
thou hast established the world
by thy wisdom,
and hast stretched out the heavens
by thy discretion.
The Lord of hosts is thy name.
—Jeremiah 10:6–16

All Nations Shall Worship

Great and marvelous are thy works,
Lord God Almighty;
just and true are thy ways,
thou King of saints.
Who shall not fear thee, O Lord,
and glorify thy name?
for thou only art holy:
for all nations shall come
and worship before thee;
for thy judgments
are made manifest.
—Revelation 15:3–4

What Is Man?

Blessed art thou, O Lord, my strength.
Thou art my goodness and my fortress,
   my high tower, and my deliverer,
   my shield, and he in whom I trust.
Lord, what is man
   that thou takest knowledge of him!
   or the son of man,
   that thou makest account of him!
          —Psalm 144:1–3

Great Art Thou, O Lord

I will extol thee, my God,
   and I will bless thy name
   for ever and ever.
   Great art thou, O Lord,
   and greatly to be praised;
   and thy greatness is unsearchable.
Thou, Lord, art gracious
   and full of compassion;
   slow to anger and of great mercy.
   Thou art good to all,
   and thy tender mercies
   are over all thy works.
Thou, O Lord, upholdest all that fall,
   and raisest up all those
   that be bowed down.
The eyes of all wait upon thee;

and thou givest them their meat
in due season.
Thou openest thine hand
and satisfiest the desire
of every living thing.
Thou art righteous in all thy ways,
and holy in all thy works.
Thou art nigh unto all them
that call upon thee,
to all that call upon thee
in truth.
                    —Psalm 145 (selected verses)

Of One Blood

Thou hast made of one blood
all nations of men
for to dwell
on all the face of the earth,
and hast determined
the times before appointed,
and the bounds of their habitation;
that they should seek thee,
if haply they might feel after thee,
and find thee,
for thou art not far
from every one of us;
for in thee we live, and move,
and have our being.
                    —Acts 17:26–28

In Perfect Peace

Thou wilt keep him in perfect peace
    whose mind is stayed on thee;
    because he trusteth in thee.
With my soul have I desired thee
    in the night;
    yea, with my spirit within me
    will I seek thee early:
    for when thy judgments
    are in the earth,
    the inhabitants of the world
    will learn righteousness.
            —Isaiah 26:3,9

I Praise Thee, O God

I praise thee, O Lord.
    I praise thy name.
    I praise thee; for thou art good.
I know that thou, O Lord, art great,
    that thou art above all gods.
Whatsoever thou didst wish to do,
    that didst thou
    in heaven and in earth,
    in the seas, and all deep places.
Thou dost cause the vapours
    to ascend from the ends
    of the earth;
    thou dost make the lightnings
    for the rain;

thou dost bring the wind
out of thy treasuries.
Thy name, O Lord,
endureth for ever.
I praise thee, O God.
—Psalm 135:3–7,13

Early Will I Seek Thee

O God, thou art my God,
early will I seek thee;
my soul thirsteth for thee,
in a dry and thirsty land
where no water is.
—Psalm 63:1

Amen

Amen: Blessing, and glory,
and wisdom, and thanksgiving,
and honour, and power, and might,
be unto thee, our God, for ever and ever. Amen.
—Revelation 7:12

Thou Art the Great, the Mighty

Ah, Lord God!
Behold, thou hast made
the heaven and the earth
by thy great power

and stretched out arm,
and there is nothing too hard for thee:
Thou showest loving kindness
unto thousands.
Thou art the Great, the Mighty,
the Lord of hosts is thy name;
great in counsel,
and mighty in work;
for thine eyes are open
upon all the ways of the sons of men;
to give everyone
according to his ways,
and according to the fruit
of his doings.
—Jeremiah 32:17–19

Of Confession and Penitence

Woe is me! for I am undone: because I am a man of
unclean lips.   —Isaiah 6:5

The immediate result of Isaiah's vision of the glory of God
was a deep conviction of his own unworthiness.

Then I said, Woe is me! for I am undone; because I am a man
of unclean lips, and I dwell in the midst of a people of unclean
lips; for mine eyes have seen the King, the Lord of hosts.
                                         —Isaiah 6:5

How odd that Isaiah's confession should concentrate on
"unclean lips" and not on some more obvious form of
evil-doing! On second thought, however, surely this is one
area where every one of us stands under condemnation. We
may not have committed murder, nor theft, nor adultery,
nor other dramatic sins, but who of us would dare claim
that "the words of our mouth" are completely acceptable to
God?

One is reminded of the passage in the New Testament
book of James:

If any man offend not in word, the same is a perfect man, and
able also to bridle the whole body.

Behold, we put bits in the horses' mouths, that they may obey us; and we turn about their whole body.

Behold also the ships, which though they be so great, and are driven of fierce winds, yet are they turned about with a very small helm, whithersoever the governor listeth.

Even so the tongue is a little member, and boasteth great things. Behold, how great a matter a little fire kindleth!

And the tongue is a fire, a world of iniquity: so is the tongue among our members, that it defileth the whole body and setteth on fire the course of nature; and it is set on fire of hell.

For every kind of beast, and of birds, and of serpents, and of things in the sea, is tamed, and hath been tamed of mankind:

But the tongue can no man tame; it is an unruly evil, full of deadly poison.

Therewith bless we God, even the Father; and therewith curse we men, which are made after the similitude of God.

Out of the same mouth proceedeth blessing and cursing. My brethren, these things ought not so to be.

Doth a fountain send forth at the same place sweet water and bitter?

Can the fig tree, my brethren, bear olive berries? either a vine figs? so can no fountain both yield salt water and fresh.

—James 3:2–12

Some of the prayers of confession in this section may become our own just as they are; or they may awaken in us an awareness of our own specific failures, of our own sins both of omission and commission, and so may lead us to genuine and particular confessions of our own.

Blot Out My Transgressions

Have mercy upon me, O God,
  according to thy loving kindness;
  according to the multitude
  of thy tender mercies,
  blot out my transgressions.
Wash me thoroughly
  from mine iniquity,
  and cleanse me from my sin.
  For I acknowledge
  my transgressions;
  and my sin is ever before me.
Against thee, thee only,
  have I sinned,
  and done this evil in thy sight.
Create in me a clean heart, O God;
  and renew a right spirit within me.
  Cast me not away from thy presence,
  and take not thy holy spirit from me.
Restore unto me
  the joy of thy salvation,
  and uphold me with thy free spirit.
      —Psalm 51:1–4,10–12

Be Merciful

God, be merciful to me
  a sinner.
            —Luke 18:13

I Grope Like the Blind

Behold, O God,
  thy hand is not shortened
  that it cannot save;
  neither is thy ear heavy
  that it cannot hear.
But my iniquities
  have separated me from thee, O God,
  and my sins have hid thy face from me.
I wait for light, but behold obscurity;
  for brightness but I walk in darkness.
  I grope for the wall like the blind,
  and I grope as if I had no eyes;
  I stumble at noonday as in the night.
My transgressions
  are multiplied before thee,
  and my sins testify against me.
But thine arm can bring salvation,
  and thy righteousness
  can sustain me.
            —Isaiah 59:1–2,9–10,16

No More Worthy

Father, I have sinned
  against heaven, and before thee,
  and am no more worthy
  to be called thy son.
        —Luke 15:18–19

In Me Dwelleth No Good Thing

I know, O God, that in me
  (that is, in my flesh)
  dwelleth no good thing:
  for to will is present with me;
  but how to perform
  that which is good I find not.
For the good that I would
  I do not;
  but the evil which I would not,
  that I do.
O wretched that I am!
  Who shall deliver me
  from the body of this death?
I thank thee, God,
  for Jesus Christ our Lord.
        —Romans 7:18–19,24–25

One Father

Art thou not the one Father of us all?
  Hast thou not created us all?
  Forgive us that we deal treacherously
  every man against his brother.
          —Malachi 2:10

We Are Thy People

We are all as an unclean thing,
  and all our righteousnesses
  are as filthy rags,
  and our iniquities, like the wind,
  have taken us away.
And there is none that
  calleth upon thy name,
  that stirreth up himself
  to take hold of thee;
  for thou hast hid thy face from us,
  and hast consumed us
  because of our iniquities.
But now, O Lord, thou art our Father;
  we are the clay, and thou our potter;
  and we are all the work of thy hand.
Be not wroth very sore, O Lord,
  neither remember iniquity for ever;
  behold, see, we beseech thee,
  we are all thy people.
          —Isaiah 64:6–8,9

Job's Prayer

I know that thou
   canst do everything,
   and that no thought
   can be withholden from thee.
I have uttered
   that I understood not;
   things too wonderful for me,
   which I knew not.
I have heard of thee
   by the hearing of the ear;
   but now mine eye seeth thee.
Wherefore I abhor myself,
   and repent in dust and ashes.
        —Job 42:1–6

I Have Rebelled Against Thee

O Lord, I have sinned,
   and have committed iniquity,
   and have done wickedly,
   and have rebelled
   even by departing
   from thy precepts
   and from thy judgments.
Neither have I hearkened
   unto the prophets
   which spake in thy name.
   But to thee, O Lord my God,

belong mercy and forgiveness,
though I have rebelled against thee.
—Daniel 9:5–6,9

Thou Knowest the Hearts

O Lord God,
there is no God like thee
in the heaven nor in the earth,
which keepest covenant
and showest mercy unto those
who walk before thee
with all their hearts.
Hearken unto the supplications
of us, thy people;
hear thou,
and when thou hearest, forgive.
And render unto every man
according unto all his ways,
whose heart thou knowest
(for thou only knowest
the hearts of the children of men).
—II Chronicles 6:14,21,30

The Words of My Mouth

Let the words of my mouth
and the meditation of my heart
be acceptable in thy sight,
O Lord, my strength
and my redeemer.
—Psalm 19:14

Out of My Distresses

The troubles of my heart
   are enlarged.
   O bring thou me
   out of my distresses.
Look upon mine affliction
   and my pain,
   and forgive all my sins.
O keep my soul, and deliver me,
   for I put my trust in thee.
            —Psalm 25:17–20

My Steps Had Slipped

Truly thou, God, art good to thy people,
   even to such as are of a clean heart.
   But as for me, my feet were almost gone;
   my steps had well nigh slipped.
   For I was envious when I saw
   the prosperity of the wicked.
So foolish was I, and ignorant,
   I was as a beast before thee.
Nevertheless,
   I am continually with thee;
   thou hast holden me by my right hand.
   Thou shalt guide me with thy counsel,
   and afterward receive me to glory.
Whom have I in heaven but thee?
   and there is none upon earth
   that I desire beside thee.

My flesh and my heart faileth,
    but thou art the strength of my heart
    and my portion for ever.
It is good for me
    to draw near to thee.
    I have put my trust
    in thee, Lord God.
            —Psalm 73:1–3,22–26,28

Assurances of Forgiveness

Thine iniquity is taken away. —Isaiah 6:7

In Peter's sermon in the third chapter of Acts, immediately following the healing of the lame beggar at the temple gate, there is a precious verse that we do well to ponder:

Repent ye, that your sins may be blotted out *when the times of refreshing shall come from the presence of the Lord.*
—Acts 3:19

The "times of refreshing" when we have the comforting assurance of God's forgiveness come "from the presence of the Lord." In Isaiah's story, he was not left to sink into despair at the bitter knowledge of his own unworthiness. God's presence was surrounding him—as it also surrounds us—"the times of refreshing" are always and instantly available. Isaiah's confession was quickly followed by an assurance of forgiveness:

Then flew one of the seraphim unto me, having a live coal in his hand, which he had taken with the tongs from off the altar:
And he laid it upon my mouth, and said, Lo, this has touched thy lips; and thine iniquity is taken away, and thy sin is purged.
—Isaiah 6:6–7

God's forgiveness is to be had for the asking, but genuine acceptance of forgiveness is sometimes difficult to achieve. Wallowing in a sense of one's own unworthiness can do nothing toward rectifying the evil already committed nor toward preventing its recurrence. The proof of true repentance is the ability to accept forgiveness (to forgive oneself) and to face life again renewed, courageous, and joyous.

How the course of history would have been changed had two of the early Christians refused to accept God's forgiveness, and remained self-condemnatory all the rest of their lives!

Consider Peter. On the fateful night of Jesus' arrest, what a coward he turned out to be. After he had "followed afar off," he finally sat down among a crowd in the hall of the high priest's house. A maid noticed him.

Maid: This man also was with him.
Peter: Woman, I know him not.

Later:

Man: Thou art also one of them.
Peter: Man, I am not!

And still later:

Man: Of a truth, this fellow also was with him, for he is a Galilaean.
Peter: Man, I know not what thou sayest.

—Luke 22:54–62

No wonder, moments later, when his eyes met those of Jesus, that Peter "went out and wept bitterly." Eventually, however, Peter was able to accept God's forgiveness, and to forgive himself, although surely he could never forget completely his denial. He did, however, find strength to go forward to years of faithful service to his beloved Lord, and to probable triumphant martyrdom.

And consider Paul. He was another man who had good reason to be crushed under a hopeless load of guilt and remorse because of his bitter persecution of the followers of Jesus in Jerusalem. In the book of Acts he is described as "breathing out threatenings and slaughter against the disciples of the Lord." (Acts 3:1.) Yet it was this same Paul after his conversion who could say:

This one thing I do, forgetting those things which are behind, and reaching forward to those things which are before, I press toward the mark for the prize of the high calling of God in Jesus Christ. —Philippians 3:13,14

All through the Bible are repeated assurances of God's readiness to forgive the sins and shortcomings of his people. A number of these are in the pages that follow.

Joy in Heaven

Jesus said:
    What man of you, having an hundred sheep,
        if he lose one of them,
        doth not leave the ninety and nine
        in the wilderness,
        and go after that which is lost,
        until he find it?
    And when he hath found it,
        he layeth it on his shoulders,
        rejoicing.
    And when he cometh home,
        he calleth together his friends
        and neighbors, saying,
        Rejoice with me:
        for I have found my sheep
        which was lost.
    I say unto you, that likewise
        joy shall be in heaven
        over one sinner that repenteth,
        more than over the ninety and nine
        which need no repentance.
            —Luke 15:4–7

I Will Hear

Thus saith the Lord:
    If my people shall humble themselves,
    and pray, and seek my face,
    and turn from their wicked ways;
    then I will hear from heaven,
    and will forgive their sin.
           —II Chronicles 7:14

I Have Redeemed Thee

Thus saith the Lord:
    Thou hast not called upon me, my child;
        but thou hast been weary of me.
        Thou hast wearied me with thine iniquities.
    I, even I, am he that blotteth out
        thy transgressions for my own sake,
        and will not remember thy sins.
    Put me in remembrance:
        let us plead together;
        declare thou,
        that thou mayest be justified.
    I have blotted out,
        as a thick cloud,
        thy transgressions,
        and as a cloud, thy sins.
    Return unto me;
        for I have redeemed thee.
           —Isaiah 43:22–26;44:22

Ready to Forgive

Unto thee, O Lord,
    do I lift up my soul.
    For thou, Lord, art good,
    and ready to forgive;
    and plenteous in mercy
    unto all them
    that call upon thee.
               —Psalm 86:4–5

White as Snow

Thus saith the Lord:
    Wash you, make you clean;
    put away the evil of your doings
    from before mine eyes;
    cease to do evil;
    learn to do well;
    seek judgment,
    relieve the oppressed,
    judge the fatherless,
    plead for the widows.
Come now, and let us reason together,
    though your sins be as scarlet,
    they shall be white as snow;
    though they be red like crimson,
    they shall be as wool.
               —Isaiah 1:16–18

The High and Lofty One

For thus saith the high and lofty One
    that inhabiteth eternity,
    whose name is Holy!
I dwell in the high and holy place,
    with him also that is
    of a contrite and humble spirit,
    to revive the spirit of the humble,
    and to revive the heart
    of the contrite ones.
          —Isaiah 57:15

Gracious and Merciful

Thou art a God
    ready to pardon,
    gracious and merciful,
    slow to anger,
    and of great kindness.
          —Nehemiah 9:17

I Acknowledged My Sin

Blessed is he whose transgression
    is forgiven.
    Blessed is the man
    unto whom thou, O God,
    imputest not iniquity,

and in whose spirit
there is no guile.
I acknowledged my sin unto thee
and mine iniquity have I not hid.
I said, I will confess
my transgression unto the Lord,
and thou forgavest
the iniquity of my sin.
—Psalm 32:1–2,5

Forsake Your Wicked Ways

Thus saith the Lord:
Seek ye me, the Lord thy God,
while I may be found:
call ye upon me
while I am near.
Forsake your wicked ways
and unrighteous thoughts,
and return to me,
and I will have mercy upon you;
for I will abundantly pardon.
—Isaiah 55:6–7

Like as a Father

Thou hast not dealt with us
after our sins;
nor rewarded us
according to our iniquities.
For as the heaven is high

above the earth,
   so great is thy mercy
   toward them that fear thee.
As far as the east is from the west,
   so far hast thou removed
   our transgressions from us.
Like as a father pitieth his children
   so thou, O Lord, dost pity
   them that fear thee.
         —Psalm 103:10–13

Into the Depths of the Sea

Who is a God like unto thee,
   that pardoneth iniquity,
   and passeth by transgressions?
Thou retainest not thine anger
   for ever because thou
   dost delight in mercy.
Thou wilt turn again,
   thou wilt have compassion on us;
   thou wilt subdue our iniquities;
   and thou wilt cast all our sins
   into the depths of the sea.
         —Micah 7:18–19

Longsuffering

Beloved, be not ignorant
   of this one thing,
   that one day is with the Lord

as a thousand years,
and a thousand years as one day.
The Lord is not slack
concerning his promise,
as some men count slackness,
but is longsuffering
to us-ward, not willing
that any should perish,
but that all should come
to repentance.
—II Peter 3:8–9

If Ye Forgive

Jesus said:
if ye forgive men
their trespasses,
your heavenly Father
will also forgive you.
—Matthew 6:14

A Broken Heart

Thus saith the Lord:
I am nigh unto them
that are of a broken heart;
and save such as be
of a contrite spirit.
—Psalm 34:18

Forgive

> Jesus said:
>> When ye stand praying,
>> forgive, if ye have
>> aught against any;
>> that your Father also
>> which is in heaven
>> may forgive you
>> your trespasses.
>>> —Mark 11:25

To Call Sinners

> Jesus said:
>> They that are whole
>> need not a physician;
>> but they that are sick.
>> I came not to call
>> the righteous, but sinners
>> to repentance.
>>> —Luke 5:31,32

Remission of Sins

> To Jesus give all the prophets
> witness, that through his name
> whosoever believeth in him
> shall receive remission of sins.
>> —Acts 10:43

Propitiation

If we sin, we have an advocate
    with the Father,
    Jesus Christ, the righteous;
    and he is the propitiation
    for our sins;
    and not for ours only,
    but also for the sins
    of the whole world.
            —I John 2:1–2

A Faithful Saying

This is a faithful saying,
    and worthy of all acceptation,
    that Christ Jesus came
    into the world to save sinners.
            —I Timothy 1:15

Covenant

Thus saith the Lord:
    This is the covenant
    that I will make with you.
    I will put my laws
    into your hearts,
    and in your minds
    will I write them;

and your sins and iniquities
will I remember no more.
      —Hebrews 10:16–17

Renewal

For we ourselves also were
    sometimes foolish, disobedient,
    deceived, serving
    divers lusts and pleasures,
    living in malice and envy,
    hateful, and hating one another.
But after the kindness and love
    of God our Saviour
    toward man appeared,
    not by works of righteousness
    which we have done,
    but according to his mercy
    he saved us,
    by the washing of regeneration,
    and renewing of the Holy Spirit,
    which he shed on us abundantly
    through Jesus Christ our Saviour.
      —Titus 3:3–6

The Blood of Jesus

These things write we unto you,
    that your joy may be full.
    This then is the message
    which we have heard

of Jesus Christ,
and declare unto you,
that God is light,
and in him is no darkness at all.
If we say
that we have fellowship with him,
and walk in darkness, we lie,
and do not the truth;
but if we walk in the light,
as he is in the light,
we have fellowship
one with another,
and the blood
of Jesus Christ his Son
cleanseth us from all sin.
—I John 1:4–7

Who Shall Stand?

If thou, Lord,
shouldest mark iniquities,
O Lord, who shall stand?
But there is forgiveness with thee.
—Psalm 130:3–4

I Will Remember No More

Thus saith the Lord:
I will be merciful
to your unrighteousness,
and your sins and iniquities
will I remember no more.
—Hebrews 8:12

Faithful and Just

If we say that we have no sin,
　　we deceive ourselves,
　　and the truth is not in us.
If we confess our sins,
　　thou art faithful and just
　　to forgive us our sins
　　and to cleanse us
　　from all unrighteousness.
　　　　　—I John 1:8–9

Good Cheer

Jesus said:
　　Be of good cheer:
　　thy sins be forgiven thee.
　　　　　—Matthew 9:2

Revive Me Again

Lord, thou hast forgiven
　　mine iniquity.
　　Thou hast covered all my sin.
Revive me again,
　　that I may rejoice in thee.
　　Show me thy mercy, O Lord,
　　and grant me thy salvation.
　　　　　—Psalm 85:2,6–7

For Grace to Hear God's Voice

I heard the voice of the Lord. —Isaiah 6:8

The purposeful focussing on the reality of God, followed by a confession of wrong-doing and an assurance of forgiveness, opens the heart to the guidance of God's indwelling Holy Spirit. God's word came to Isaiah through a vision in which he heard a voice. Sometimes we wish that God would speak to us as clearly as he seems to have spoken to the Bible people.

A favorite Bible story having to do with God's communication with men is that of Elijah at Mt. Horeb, hiding from the wrath of Jezebel:

And he came thither unto a cave, and lodged there; and behold, the word of the Lord came to him, and he said unto him, What doest thou here, Elijah?

And he said, I have been very jealous for the Lord God of hosts; for the children of Israel have forsaken thy covenant, thrown down thy altars, and slain thy prophets with the sword; and I, even I only, am left; and they seek my life to take it away.

And he said, Go forth, and stand upon the mount before the Lord. And, behold, the Lord passed by, and a great and strong wind rent the mountains, and brake in pieces the rocks before the Lord: but the Lord was not in the wind: and after the wind an earthquake; but the Lord was not in the earthquake;

And after the earthquake a fire; but the Lord was not in the fire; and after the fire a still small voice.

And the Lord said unto Elijah, Go, return on thy way. Yet have I left me seven thousand in Israel, all the knees that have not bowed unto Baal. —I Kings 19:9–12,18

Those who have ears to hear, are still aware of the still small voice, but there are other ways in which God speaks today. Sometimes God speaks through nature:

The heavens declare the glory of God; and the firmament showeth his handiwork.

Day unto day uttereth speech, and night unto night showeth knowledge. —Psalm 19:1–2

God spoke to the Hebrews through the star-sprinkled sky. They had no knowledge of the vast reaches of the universe. They did not know that beyond the farthest star they could see, were millions of other stars; or that the light from the stars had traveled uncounted years before it reached our earth. But still as they lifted their eyes to the stars, God spoke to them of the mystery and power of creation.

God still speaks to us through the marvels of his creation. Our greater knowledge only reveals more and more of the mysteries and wonders of this strange universe. God speaks through the starry skies, through the perfect geometric forms of tiny snowflakes, through the pulsing life in dead-looking seeds, through the mysterious life in our own bodies. He is saying:

I am the Lord, and there is none else, there is no God beside me. I form the light, and create darkness.

I have made the earth, and created man upon it: I, even my hands, have stretched out the heavens, and all their host have I commanded. —Isaiah 45:5,7,12

Sometimes God speaks through a picture. During World War II, a newspaper photographer snapped a picture, showing a tiny baby, screaming his heart out, all alone. Around him were the ruins of a city. Hundreds of people had been killed in an atom bomb explosion, but somehow this small boy had lived through it. Nothing else in the picture was alive—just this tiny boy, hurt and terrified, and alone.

The photographer sent his picture to a newspaper. It was published again and again. Hundreds and thousands of people saw it. And through this picture God spoke clearly and unmistakably:

They shall beat their swords into plowshares, and their spears into pruning-hooks; nation shall not lift up sword against nation, neither shall they learn war any more.

But they shall sit every man under his vine and under his fig tree, and none shall make them afraid; for the mouth of the Lord of hosts hath spoken it. Micah 4:3–4

And thousands of persons heard God's voice and consecrated themselves to renewed efforts to end the futility and stupidity of war.

Sometimes God speaks through television. An earthquake or a disastrous tidal wave occurs; and in comfortable, safe living rooms around the world people see the tragedy and suffering in front of their very eyes—and countless people in far-scattered places give of their substance to care for human need in response to God's call.

One thing is sure, God is speaking to us today in these and many diverse ways, as surely as he ever spoke to our forefathers. Thousands of witnesses across the world can testify that direct guidance still comes in every area of their lives. The indwelling Spirit of God, and the Word of God in the Scriptures, still actively and positively guide those who commit themselves to the Christ of God.

Grant That I May Hearken

Grant that I may hearken
  unto thy voice;
  that thou wilt give me counsel;
  that thou wilt be with me.
      —Exodus 18:19

Thou Wilt Speak Peace

I will hear what thou, O God,
  wilt speak, for thou wilt
  speak peace to us.
  Surely thy salvation is nigh to us
  that glory may dwell in us.
      —Psalm 85:8–9

My Hard Heart

Grant, O God, that today
  I may hear thy voice
  and harden not my heart.
      —Psalm 95:7–8

To Do That Which Is Right

Give us grace
to hearken to thy voice, O God:
to keep all thy commandments;
to do that which is right
in thine eyes, O Lord our God.
—Deuteronomy 13:18

By My Spirit

Grant us to hear and understand
thy word to us:
Not by might, nor by power,
but by my spirit
shalt thou overcome.
—Zechariah 4:6

Thy Word in My Heart

With my whole heart
have I sought thee;
O let me not wander
from thy commandments.
Thy word have I hid in my heart,
that I might not sin
against thee.
Blessed art thou, O Lord,

teach me thy statutes.
Open thou mine eyes
that I may behold
wondrous things out of thy law.
   —Psalm 119:10–12,18

Stablish Thy Word

Teach me, O Lord,
 the way of thy statutes
 and I shall keep it
 unto the end.
Give me understanding
 and I shall keep thy law;
 yea, I shall observe it
 with my whole heart.
Make me to go
 in the path
 of thy commandments;
 for therein do I delight.
Stablish thy word unto me.
   —Psalm 119:33–35,38

The Knock at the Door

Grant, O Lord, that as thou standest
 and knockest at the door,
I may hear thy voice
and open the door to thee.
   —Revelation 3:20

With All My Heart

I have hearkened to thy voice,
    O Lord my God;
    give me grace to keep and do
    all thy commandments
    with all my heart
    and with all my soul.
            —Deuteronomy 26:14,17

Of Commitment and Dedication

Here am I. Send me. —Isaiah 6:8

Isaiah heard God's call to service and responded with a brief five words—and the commitment of the rest of his life.

A great deal is said and written about *God's answer* to prayer (or the lack of it). Seldom, however, is *our answer* to God given the same amount of consideration. And yet every true experience of prayer that achieves genuine communication with God includes some specific suggestion and guidance on his part to which an answer is required.

It is not, of course, always a challenge to a major decision that will change the course of a life (although Isaiah's experience has been duplicated untold numbers of times). Sometimes our confession may concern intimate family relationships where we have miserably failed to live up to the best we know. And the assurance of forgiveness that lightens our hearts is always accompanied by a directive:

Neither do I condemn thee. Go and sin no more.   —John 8:11

Or our confession may have to do with a deliberate sin of "unclean lips"—we may have been guilty of repeating unconfirmed gossip—and the assurance of forgiveness may be followed by guidance as to how partially to undo the mischief we have caused.

Or our confession may concern the neglect of an obvious duty—a letter that should have been written, a phone call that should have been made, a neighbor in trouble who should have been visited. The assurance of God's forgiveness is comforting, but God's voice does not stop with the assurance: it adds a "go," "do," "act," "give," "love."

When we really hear and understand God's voice, we have two choices: we can say, "No, I won't," or "Yes, Lord, yes, I will."

Search Me, O God

O Lord, thou hast searched me
   and known me.
      Thou knowest my downsitting
      and mine uprising;
      thou understandest my thought
      afar off.
Thou compassest my path
      and my lying down,
         and art acquainted with all my ways;
         for there is not a word in my tongue
         but thou knowest it altogether.
Such knowledge is too wonderful
      for me; it is high;
      I cannot attain unto it.
      I will praise thee for I am
      fearfully and wonderfully made.
How precious also are thy thoughts
      unto me, O God!
      How great is the sum of them!
Search me, O God, and know my heart;
      and see if there be
      any wicked way in me,
         and lead me in the way everlasting.
                  —Psalm 139:1–6,14–24

What Dost Thou Require?

Wherewith shall I come before thee,
  Lord, and bow myself before thee,
  O God most high?
Shall I come before thee
  with burnt offerings,
  with calves a year old?
  Wilt thou be pleased
  with thousands of rams,
  or with ten thousands
  of rivers of oil?
  Shall I give my first born
  for my transgression,
  the fruit of my body
  for the sin of my soul?
Thou hast shown us, O God, what is good;
  and what dost thou require of us
  but to do justly,
  and to love mercy,
  and to walk humbly with thee?
          —Micah 6:6–8

The Door of My Lips

Set a watch, O Lord,
  before my mouth;
  keep thou the door of my lips.
          —Psalm 141:3

Thy Kingdom First

Give us grace, O God,
    to take no thought, saying,
    What shall we eat?
    or What shall we drink?
    or Wherewithal shall we be clothed?
For thou, heavenly Father,
    knowest that we have need
    of all these things.
Grant us
    to seek first thy kingdom
    and thy righteousness,
    knowing that then
    all these things
    will be added unto us.
                —Matthew 6:31–33

The Mind of Jesus Christ

Let this mind be in us, O God,
    which was also in Christ Jesus.
    For it is thou
    who workest in us
    both to will and to do
    of thy good pleasure.
                —Philippians 2:5,13

Children of Thine

Grant us grace, holy Father,
  to love our enemies,
  to bless them that curse us,
  to do good to them that hate us,
  and to pray for them
  which despitefully use us
  and persecute us,
  that we may be children of thine,
  our heavenly Father,
  for thou makest thy sun to rise
  on the evil and on the good,
  and sendest rain
  on the just and on the unjust.
            —Matthew 5:44–45

Make Us Perfect

God of peace, who brought again
  from the dead, our Lord Jesus,
  that great shepherd of the sheep,
  make us perfect
  in every good work to do thy will,
  working in us that
  which is well pleasing in thy sight,
  through Jesus Christ our Lord,
  to whom be glory for ever and ever. Amen.
            —Hebrews 13:20–21

To Hold Fast Our Faith

Enable us, O God, to hold fast our faith
   without wavering (for thou art faithful
   to thy promises);
   and grant that we may consider
   one another, to provoke unto love
   and to good works,
   not forsaking the assembling
   of ourselves together,
   but exhorting one another.
And grant us grace to offer
   the sacrifice of praise to thee,
   O God, continually,
   the fruit of our lips
   giving thanks to thy name.
           —Hebrews 10:23–25;13:15

With All Our Hearts

Give us grace to love thee,
   O Lord our God,
   with all our hearts,
   and with all our souls,
   and with all our minds—
   and our neighbor
   as ourselves.
          —Matthew 22:37–39

Unto Thy Glory

Grant, O God, that our love
    may abound yet more and more
    in knowledge and in all judgment;
    that we may approve
    all things that are excellent,
    that we may be sincere
    and without offence;
    being filled with the fruits
    of righteousness
    which are by Jesus Christ,
    unto thy glory and praise, O God.
            —Philippians 1:9–11

A Sanctified Vessel

Give me grace, Lord, to be strong;
    to endure hardness as a good soldier
    of Jesus Christ.
    Make me a workman approved by thee,
    who need not be ashamed.
Give me understanding of thy word.
Make me a vessel, sanctified,
    and fit for thy use,
    prepared for every good work.
            —II Timothy 2:1–3,15,21

That Christ May Dwell in Our Hearts

For this cause we bow our knees
    unto thee, O God,
    that thou wilt grant us
    according to the riches of thy glory
    to be strengthened with might
    by thy Spirit in the inner man,
    that Christ may dwell in our hearts
    by faith, that we,
    being rooted and grounded in love,
    may be able to comprehend
    with all the saints,
    what is the breadth and length,
    and depth and height,
    and to know the love of Christ
    which passeth knowledge,
    that we may be filled
    with all thy fulness, O God.
            —Ephesians 3:14–19

Forbearing One Another in Love

We beseech thee, O God,
    that we may walk worthy
    of the vocation
    wherewith we are called,
    with all lowliness and meekness,
    with longsuffering,
    forbearing one another in love,

endeavoring to keep
the unity of the Spirit
in the bond of peace.
　　　　—Ephesians 4:1–3

Treasures in Heaven

Give us grace, O God,
　　not to lay up for ourselves
　　treasures upon earth,
　　where moth and rust doth corrupt,
　　and where thieves
　　break through and steal:
　　but to lay up for ourselves
　　treasures in heaven,
　　where neither moth nor rust
　　doth corrupt, and where thieves
　　do not break through and steal.
　　　　—Matthew 6:19–20

Tenderhearted, Forgiving

Give us strength, O God,
　　to put away from us
　　all bitterness and wrath,
　　and anger, and clamor,
　　and evil speaking, with all malice.
Grant us grace
　　to be kind, one to another,
　　tenderhearted, forgiving
　　one another, even as thou,

for Christ's sake,
hast forgiven us.
—Ephesians 4:31–32

In All Our Tribulations

Blessed be thou, O God,
  the Father of our Lord
  Jesus Christ,
  the Father of mercies,
  and the God of all comfort,
  who comfortest us
  in all our tribulation,
  that we may be able
  to comfort them
  which are in any trouble,
  by the comfort
  wherewith we ourselves
  are comforted by thee, O God.
      —II Corinthians 1:3–4

Thy Statutes Are Right

Thy law, O God, is perfect,
  converting the soul;
  thy testimony is sure,
  making wise the simple.
Thy statutes are right,
  rejoicing the heart;
  thy commandment is pure,
  enlightening the eyes.

The fear of thee, O God, is clean,
   enduring forever;
     thy judgments are true
     and righteous altogether.
     More to be desired are they
     than gold, yea, than much fine gold;
     sweeter also than honey
     and the honeycomb;
     and in keeping of them
     there is great reward.
Who can understand his errors?
   cleanse thou me from secret faults.
   Keep me back also from
   presumptuous sins;
     let them not have dominion over me.
Let the words of my mouth,
   and the meditation of my heart
   be acceptable in thy sight,
     O Lord, my strength and my redeemer.
             —Psalm 19:7–14

Whatsoever Things Are True

Grant us grace, O God,
   to fill our hearts and minds
   with whatsoever things are true,
   whatsoever things are honest,
   whatsoever things are just,
   whatsoever things are pure,
   whatsoever things are lovely,
   whatsoever things are of good report.
          —Philippians 4:8

In Whatsoever State I Am

Grant, our Father, that I may learn
 in whatsoever state I am
 therewith to be content;
 that I may know
 both how to be abased,
 and how to abound;
 and how to suffer need.
And grant me faith to know
 that I can do all things
 through Christ
 who strengtheneth me.
    —Philippians 4:11–13

A Living Sacrifice

Strengthen me, by thy mercy, O God,
 that I may present my body
 a living sacrifice,
 holy, acceptable unto thee,
 which is my reasonable service.
And let me not be conformed
 to this world,
 but be transformed
 by the renewing of my mind,
 that I may prove
 what is thy good and acceptable
 and perfect will.
And having gifts which thou hast given me,

enable me to use them fervently,
serving thee, O Lord;
rejoicing in hope,
patient in tribulation,
continuing instant in prayer.
—Romans 12:1–2,6,11–12

Peace in Believing

Now, God of hope, fill us
with all joy and peace in believing,
that we may abound in hope
through the power of the Holy Spirit.
—Romans 15:13

The Love That Suffereth Long

Give us grace, O loving God,
to love with the love
that suffereth long,
and is kind;
that envieth not;
that vaunteth not itself;
is not puffed up;
that doth not behave itself unseemly;
seeketh not her own,
is not easily provoked,
thinketh no evil;
that rejoiceth not in iniquity,
but rejoiceth in the truth;
beareth all things,

believeth all things,
hopeth all things,
endureth all things;
the love that never faileth.
—I Corinthians 13:4–8

The Fruit of the Spirit

Produce in me, O God, I pray
the fruit of the Spirit:
love, joy, peace, longsuffering,
gentleness, goodness, faith,
meekness, temperance.
—Galatians 5:22–23

As Thine Elect

Grant that we may put on,
as thine elect, O God,
holy and beloved,
mercy, kindness, humbleness
of mind, meekness,
longsuffering;
forbearing one another,
and forgiving one another,
even as Christ forgives us.
And may thy peace
rule in our hearts,
and may the word of Christ
dwell in us richly
in all wisdom;

teaching and admonishing
one another in psalms and hymns,
and spiritual songs,
singing with grace in our hearts
to thee, O Lord.
And whatsoever we do in word or deed,
grant us to do all
in the name of the Lord Jesus,
giving thanks to thee, O God.
—Colossians 3:12–13,15–17

To Delight in Thy Law

Grant us grace
not to walk in the counsel
of the ungodly, nor to stand
in the way of sinners,
nor to sit in the seat
of the scornful;
but to delight in thy law, O God,
and in thy law to meditate
day and night.
For thou, O Lord,
knowest the way of the righteous
but the way of the ungodly
shall perish.
—Psalm 1:1–2,6

In Deed and Truth

Grant us grace, holy Father,
 not to love in word,
 neither in tongue,
 but in deed and truth.
            —I John 3:18

In Full Assurance

Grant that we may draw near
 to thee, O God, with a true heart,
 in full assurance of faith.
            —Hebrews 10:22

As Yesterday

Lord, a thousand years
 in thy sight
 are but as yesterday
 when it is past,
 and as a watch in the night . . .
So teach us to number our days
 that we may apply our hearts
 unto wisdom.
            —Psalm 90:4,12

The Work of Our Hands

Let thy beauty,
    O Lord our God,
    be upon us;
    and establish thou
    the work of our hands
    upon us;
    yea, the work of our hands
    establish thou it.
                —Psalm 90:17

Doers of the Word

Grant, O God,
    that we may truly be
    doers of the word,
    and not hearers only.
                —James 1:22

Our Labor Is Not in Vain

Grant that we may be stedfast,
    unmoveable, always abounding
    in thy work, O Lord,
    knowing that our labor
    for thee is never in vain.
                —I Corinthians 15:58

For Times of Crisis

Out of the depths have I cried unto thee, O God.

—Psalm 130:1

Someone once said, "There are no atheists in fox-holes." Surely when the tragedies of life threaten to overwhelm us, when our human resources prove unequal to our desperate need, when the recognition of our utter helplessness floods our hearts with despair—then even confirmed and stubborn atheists find themselves crying out to the God whose very existence their reason has denied.

And the witness of innumerable Spirit-filled Christians throughout all ages, testifies to the truth that awareness of God's intimate presence enables one to endure courageously, without panic, even with a joyous sense of acceptance, the worst that life can do; and that the greater sense of complete dependence on God, complete trust in his sufficiency for every need, is one of the rich values growing out of times of heartbreak and tribulation.

Though I walk through the valley of the shadow of death, I will fear no evil, *for thou art with me*.   —Psalm 23:4

It is to be noted that God's presence does not prevent the trials and catastrophes from happening; it provides strength and courage to meet them triumphantly.

Thou Hast Redeemed Me

In thee, O God, do I put my trust;
    deliver me in thy righteousness.
    Bow down thine ear to me;
    deliver me speedily.
    Be thou my strong rock.
    For thy name's sake,
    lead me and guide me.
Into thine hand I commit my spirit;
    thou hast redeemed me.
    Lord God of truth,
    I trust in thee, O Lord.
    I will be glad
    and rejoice in thy mercy,
    for thou hast considered my troubles;
    thou hast known my soul
    in adversities.
                —Psalm 31:1–7

A Very Present Help

Thou, O God,
    art our refuge and strength,
    a very present help in trouble.

Therefore we will not fear,
   though the earth be removed,
   and though the mountains
   be carried into the midst of the sea;
   though the waters thereof
   roar and be troubled,
   though the mountains shake
   with the swelling thereof.
Thou, Lord, art with us;
   thou, God, art our refuge.
            —Psalm 46:1–3,7

Let Thy Mercy Be Upon Us

Behold, thine eye, O Lord,
   is upon them that love thee;
   upon them that hope in thy mercy.
   Our soul waiteth for thee, O Lord;
   thou art our help and our shield.
   For our heart shall rejoice in thee,
   because we have trusted in thy name.
Let thy mercy, O Lord, be upon us,
   according as we hope in thee.
            —Psalm 33:18–22

My Soul Thirsteth for Thee

As the hart panteth
   after the water brooks,
   so panteth my soul
   after thee, O God.

My soul thirsteth for thee,
   for thee, the living God.
My tears have been my meat
   continually, day and night;
   while they continually say unto me,
   Where is thy God?
Why am I cast down,
   and why am I disquieted within me?
   My hope is in thee, O God;
   for I shall yet praise thee
   for the help of thy countenance.
Thou, Lord, wilt command
   thy loving kindness
   in the daytime,
   and in the night thy song
   shall be with me,
   and my prayer shall be unto thee,
   O God of my life.
            —Psalm 42:1–5,8

My Times Are in Thy Hand

Have mercy upon me, O God,
   for I am in trouble;
   mine eye is consumed with grief,
   and my years with sighing;
   my strength faileth
   because of mine iniquity.
But I trusted in thee, O Lord.
   I said, Thou art my God.
   My times are in thy hand.

Make thy face to shine upon me,
for thy mercies' sake.
O how great is thy goodness,
which thou hast laid up
for them which love thee.
Blessed be thou, O Lord,
for I said in my haste,
I am cut off from before thine eyes;
nevertheless, thou heardest
the voice of my supplications
when I cried unto thee.
Thou, Lord, preservest the faithful.
Give me good courage,
and strengthen my heart,
for my hope is in thee, O Lord.
—Psalm 31:9–24

When I Cried Unto Thee

My God, my God,
why hast thou forsaken me?
why art thou so far
from helping me?
O my God, I cry in the day time,
but thou hearest not;
and in the night season,
and am not silent.
But thou art holy, O God;
our fathers trusted in thee;
they trusted, and thou
didst deliver them.

They cried unto thee
 and were delivered;
 they trusted in thee,
 and were not confounded.
Be not far from me,
 for trouble is near;
 for there is none to help.
 Be not thou far from me, O Lord;
 O my strength, make haste to help me.
I praise thee, O God;
I glorify thee, and worship thee.
 For thou hast not despised
 nor abhorred my affliction;
 neither hast thou
 hid thy face from me;
 but when I cried unto thee,
 thou heardest.
    —Psalm 22:1–5,11,19–24

I Will Not Fear

I will be strong
 and of a good courage.
 I will not fear
 nor be afraid;
 for it is thou,
 my Lord and my God,
 thou it is who goest with me.
Thou wilt not fail me
 nor forsake me.
    —Deuteronomy 31:6

Be Merciful Unto Me, O God

Be merciful unto me, O God,
    be merciful unto me;
    for my soul trusteth in thee;
    yea, in the shadow of thy wings
    will I make my refuge,
    until these calamities be overpast.
I will cry unto thee, O God most high,
    unto thee who performest
    all things for me;
    for thy mercy is great
    unto the heavens,
    and thy truth unto the clouds.
    Let thy glory be above all the earth.
            —Psalms 57:1–2,10–11

My Soul Waiteth

Truly my soul waiteth upon thee,
    O God; from thee cometh
    my salvation.
    Thou only art my rock
    and my salvation;
    thou art my defence;
    I shall not be moved.
In thee is my salvation
    and my glory;
    the rock of my strength
    and my refuge
    is in thee, O God.
            —Psalm 62:1–2,7

I Will Not Be Afraid

Thou, O Lord, art a shield for me,
    my glory, and the lifter up
    of my head.
I cried unto thee with my voice,
    and thou heardest me
    out of thy holy hill.
I laid me down and slept;
    I awaked; for thou, Lord,
    sustained me.
I will not be afraid
    of ten thousand people,
    that have set themselves
    against me round about.
Arise, O Lord,
    save me, O my God.
    Salvation belongeth unto thee,
    O God, thy blessing is upon us,
    thy people.
            —Psalm 3:3–8

Thy Secret Place

When I dwell in thy secret place,
    O most High, I abide under thy shadow,
    O Almighty.
I will say of thee, Lord,
    thou art my refuge and my fortress,
    my God, in thee will I trust.
    Surely, thou wilt deliver me
    from the snare of the fowler,

and from the noisome pestilence.
Thou wilt cover me with thy feathers,
and under thy wings will I trust;
thy truth shall be
my shield and buckler.
I will not be afraid
for the terror by night,
nor for the arrow that flieth by day,
nor for the pestilence
that walketh in darkness,
nor for the destruction
that wasteth at noonday.
Because I have set my love upon thee,
therefore wilt thou deliver me.
I will call upon thee,
and thou wilt answer me.
Thou wilt be with me in trouble.
Thou wilt deliver me.
　　　　　—Psalm 91:1–6,14–16

Why Am I Disquieted?

Why am I cast down?
and why am I disquieted
within me?
My hope is in thee,
and I shall yet praise thee,
who art the health
of my countenance,
and my God.
　　　　　—Psalm 43:5

Out of Trouble

Hear my prayer, O Lord,
    give ear to my supplications:
    in thy faithfulness answer me,
    and in thy righteousness.
    For the enemy hath persecuted my soul;
    he hath smitten my life down to the ground;
    he hath made me to dwell in darkness.
I stretch forth my hands unto thee;
    my soul thirsteth after thee
    as a thirsty land.
Hear me speedily, O God:
    my spirit faileth.
    Hide not thy face from me.
    Cause me to hear thy loving kindness
    in the morning; for in thee do I trust.
    Cause me to know the way
    wherein I should walk;
    for I lift up my soul unto thee.
Deliver me, O Lord, from my enemies;
    I flee unto thee to hide me.
    Teach me to do thy will
    for thou art my God.
Quicken me, O Lord, for thy name's sake;
    for thy righteousness' sake
    bring my soul out of trouble.
        —Psalm 143:1,3–11

Thy Armor

Grant us grace
    to be strong in thee, O Lord,
    and in the power of thy might.
Grant us grace
    to put on thy whole armor
    that we may be able to stand
    against the wiles of the devil.
    For we wrestle not against flesh and blood,
    but against principalities, against powers,
    against the rulers of darkness of this world,
    against spiritual wickedness in high places
Wherefore we take unto us thy whole armor,
    O God, that we may be able to withstand
    in the evil day,
    and having done all, to stand.
We stand, therefore, having our loins
    girt about with truth,
    and having on the breastplate
    of righteousness,
    and our feet shod with the preparation
    of the gospel of peace;
    above all, taking the shield of faith,
    wherewith we shall be able to quench
    all the fiery darts of the wicked.
    And we take the helmet of salvation,
    and the sword of the spirit,
    which is thy Word, O God.
            —Ephesians 6:10–17

My Sins Are Not Hid

O God, thou knowest my foolishness,
and my sins are not hid from thee.
Deliver me out of the mire
and let me not sink.
Let not the waterfloods overflow me,
neither let the deep swallow me up.
Hear me, O Lord,
for thy lovingkindness is good;
turn unto me
according to the multitude
of thy tender mercies,
and hide not thy face from me,
for I am in trouble.
Hear me speedily.
—Psalm 69:5,14–17

I Will Never Forsake Thee

Thou, Lord, hast said,
I will never leave thee
nor forsake thee.
Thou, Lord, art my helper,
and I will not fear
what man shall do unto me.
—Hebrews 13:5–6

Out of the Depths

Out of the depths
　　have I cried unto thee, O Lord.
　　If thou, Lord,
　　shouldest mark iniquities,
　　O Lord, who shall stand?
But there is forgiveness with thee.
I wait for thee, O Lord,
　　my soul doth wait,
　　and in thy word do I hope.
　　My soul waiteth for thee
　　more than they that watch
　　for the morning.
With thee, O God, there is mercy,
　　and with thee is plenteous redemption.
　　Thou wilt redeem us
　　from all our iniquities.
　　　　　　—Psalm 130:1–2,5–8

Thou Hast Heard My Voice

Mine enemies have cut off my life
　　in the dungeon,
　　and cast a stone upon me.
　　Waters flowed over mine head;
　　then I said, I am cut off.
I called upon thy name, O Lord,
　　out of the low dungeon.
　　Thou hast heard my voice;

hide not thine ear
  at my breathing, at my cry.
Thou drewest near in the day
  that I called upon thee;
  thou saidst, Fear not.
O Lord, thou hast redeemed my life.
          —Lamentations 3:53–58

Jesus' Prayer in Gethsemane

O my Father,
  if it be possible,
  let this cup pass from me:
  nevertheless, not as I will,
  but as thou wilt.
          —Matthew 26:39

Mine Iniquities Are Heavy

O Lord, there is no rest for me
  because of my sin.
  For mine iniquities
  are gone over my head;
  as an heavy burden
  they are too heavy for me.
  I am troubled;
  I am bowed down greatly,
  I go mourning all the day long.
In thee, O Lord, do I hope.
  Thou wilt hear, O Lord my God,

for I will declare mine iniquity.
I will be sorry for my sins.
Forsake me not, O God.
O my God, be not far from me.
Make haste to help me,
O Lord, my salvation.
—Psalm 38 (selected verses)

My Days Are Like a Shadow

Hear my prayer, O Lord,
and let my cry come unto thee.
Hide not thy face from me,
in the day when I am in trouble.
My heart is smitten
and withered like grass,
so that I forget to eat my bread.
My days are like a shadow
that declineth.
But thou, O Lord, shalt endure forever;
and thy remembrance
with all generations.
Thou wilt regard the prayer
of the destitute.
Thou hast looked down from the heaven
to behold the earth;
to hear the groaning
of the prisoner.
Of old thou hast laid the foundation
of the earth; and the heavens
are the work of thy hands.

They shall perish
but thou shalt endure;
yea, all of them shall wax old
like a garment;
as a vesture shalt thou change them,
and they shall be changed.
But thou art the same,
and thy years shall have no end.
—Psalm 102:1–2,4,11–12,17–27

When My Father and My Mother Forsake Me

Hear, O Lord,
when I cry with my voice;
have mercy also upon me,
and answer me.
When thou saidst,
Seek ye my face,
my heart said unto thee,
Thy face, Lord, will I seek.
Hide not thy face far from me;
thou hast been my help;
leave me not, neither forsake me,
O God of my salvation.
When my father and my mother
forsake me, then thou, O Lord,
wilt take me up.
—Psalm 27:7–10

The Everlasting Arms

There is none like unto thee, O God.
Thou, O eternal God, art my refuge,
and underneath
are the everlasting arms.
—Deuteronomy 33:26–27

For Others

Grant us grace to pray for one another, knowing that effective fervent prayer availeth much.   —James 5:16

Many people question the rationality and effectiveness of prayers for others. They can accept, tentatively, the fact that prayer can produce changes in the pray-er, but beyond that they are sceptical. They argue: "If God's love and concern are surrounding every individual, why is intercessory prayer necessary? Surely God knows the needs of each person and is far more eager to meet those needs than I could possibly be. Why should I ask him to do what he is already eager to do? And how can my asking have any effect?" On first thought that seems a reasonable point of view. It does, however, seem to imply a certain lack of humility, a refusal to accept the example and the explicit teaching of Jesus.

Even on a strictly "reasonable" basis, however, perhaps there is something more to be said. Surely it is true that God loves each of his created children. Think of his Spirit as a conscious, living magnet, powerfully drawing to himself the love of each individual person. But just as the force of a magnet can be blocked by inserting between the magnet and an object certain non-conductive obstacles, so perhaps the magnetic power of God's redeeming love may at times be rendered temporarily ineffective by the presence in a person of self-centeredness, indifference, or other forms of sin, or even by mere ignorance. Could it be possible that in some mysterious way intercessory prayer may provide a way to channel the power of God's love *around* the obstruction? Standing spiritually close to the person for whom we are praying, but being ourselves wide open to God and outside of the particular area of blockage, may it not be possible for God to exert *through us* his healing and redemptive power?

Prayer may be in very truth *the* most important part of our ministry to others.

As each of us has received the gift of thine indwelling Spirit, grant us to minister one to another as good stewards of thy varied grace. —I Peter 4:10

The prayers gathered in this section are necessarily impersonal. It is presumed that the person using them will insert at some point the name(s) of the person(s) for whom the prayers are offered. Moreover, these prayers are merely suggestions and introductions, to be followed, of course, by specific petitions relevant to the particular conditions surrounding the object of the prayer.

Stablish His Heart

Grant, O God,
    that this child of thine
    may increase and abound in love
    toward all men,
    to the end that thou mayest
    stablish his heart
    unblameable in holiness
    before thee.
              —I Thessalonians 3:12–13

Grow in Grace

Grant, our Father,
    that this child of thine
    may grow in grace
    and in the knowledge
    of our Lord and Saviour
    Jesus Christ.
To him be glory
    now and forever. Amen.
              —II Peter 3:18

By Thine Indwelling Spirit

For this cause I pray unto thee,
   O God, the Father
   of our Lord Jesus Christ,
   that thou wilt grant
   to this child of thine
   according to the riches of thy glory,
   to be strengthened with might
   by thine indwelling Spirit,
   that Christ may dwell in his heart
   by faith, so that he,
   being rooted and grounded in love,
   may know the love of Christ
   which passeth all knowledge
   and may be filled
   with all thy fulness.
          —Ephesians 3:14–19

Perfect in Every Good Work

Make this child of thine, O God,
   perfect in every good work
   to do thy will,
   working in him
   that which is well-pleasing
   in thy sight,
   through Jesus Christ
   to whom be glory
   for ever and ever. Amen.
          —Hebrews 13:21

Mercy and Peace

Grace be with this child of thine,
    O God, and mercy and peace
    from thee, our Father, and from
    the Lord Jesus Christ, thy Son.
                —II John 3

Follow the Good

Grant, our Father,
    that this child of thine
    may follow not
    that which is evil,
    but that which is good;
    for he that doeth good
    is of thee,
    but he that doeth evil
    hath not seen thee.
                —III John 11

Comfort His Heart

Now, God our Father,
    thou who hast loved
    this thy child,
    and hast given him
    everlasting consolation,

and good hope through grace,
comfort his heart,
and stablish him
in every good word and work.
                    —II Thessalonians 2:16–17

Love Not the World

Grant, our Father,
    that this thy child may learn
    to love not the world
    neither the things
    that are in the world,
    for if anyone love the world,
    thy love is not in him:
    for the world passeth away,
    but he that doeth thy will,
    O Father, abideth for ever.
                    —I John 2:15,17

Of Thankfulness

Fill us with thy Spirit so that we may give thanks always for all things unto thee, our Father, in the name of our Lord Jesus Christ. —Ephesians 5:18–20

The prayer of thankfulness seems at first to present the least difficulty to the beginning pray-er. How easy it is in quiet times of peace and joy to lift the heart in gratitude to the Source of all our blessings! But this is only the first step in learning to live life in a constant, unwavering spirit of thankfulness.

As the Devil well knows, it is not in times of quiet happiness and well-being that the reality of our thankfulness is tested. Do you remember in the first chapter of the book of Job, Satan's challenge to God?

And the Lord said unto Satan, Hast thou considered my servant Job, a perfect and an upright man, one that feareth God?

Then Satan answered the Lord, and said, Doth Job fear God for nought?

Hast thou not made an hedge about him, and about his house, and about all that he hath on every side? thou hast blessed the work of his hands, and his substance is increased in the land.

But put forth thy hand now, and touch all that he hath, and he will curse thee to thy face. —Job 1:9–11

How sadly we recognize in ourselves the tendency to be grateful only for those things which bring us momentary satisfaction, and how slowly we learn to "give thanks always for all things."

Theoretically, we recognize the truth symbolized by the sand in the oyster: it is the minute grain of sand within the shell, unwelcome and irritating, which produces in the course of time the lustrous, perfect pearl. So in our lives, as we look back over the years, we can see the precious values that have come out of the very trials and tribulations through which we so reluctantly passed—the illnesses, the disappointments, the economic crises, the family estrangements, the failures, the disloyalty of a trusted friend—all the long list of woes. But it is one thing to look back on past trials, and recognize thankfully blessings that have come as a result of them, but it is quite a different thing to thank God in the midst of them.

And yet, should we not in fact, be thankful for those tragic experiences which teach us what is needful for the salvation of our souls? For those which, accepted as from God's hand, develop in us those Christlike qualities, for the growth of which all life seems to be designed? For those which force on us the recognition of our complete dependence on God's love and awaken in us the realization of his complete sufficiency to meet every need?

What amazing new depths of joyous living are available to us when we achieve this much-to-be-desired ability "to give thanks to God always for all things"—to accept life in its totality from God's hands, and to thank him for *life*— its joys, its sorrows, its triumphs, its failures, its evil and its good—to praise God in the midst of it, as the continuing Creator and Sustainer of our very being!

A Good Thing

> It is a good thing to give thanks
>   unto thee, O Lord,
>   and to sing praises to thy name,
>   O most High;
>   to show forth thy lovingkindness
>   in the morning,
>   and thy faithfulness every night.
>   —Psalm 92:1–2

Let the Earth Be Glad

> Thou, Lord, art great,
>   and greatly to be praised.
>   Honour and majesty are before thee;
>   strength and beauty
>   are in thy sanctuary.
> Let the heavens rejoice
>   and let the earth be glad;
>   let the sea roar
>   and the fulness thereof.
>   Let the field be joyful
>   and all that is therein;

then shall all the trees of the wood
rejoice before thee, O Lord:
for thou comest,
for thou comest to judge the earth:
and thou shalt judge the world
with righteousness,
and the people with thy truth.
          —Psalm 96:4,6–13

While I Have My Being

I will sing unto thee, O God,
    as long as I live;
    I will sing praises to thee, my God,
    while I have my being.
My meditation of thee shall be sweet;
    I will be glad in thee, O God.
          —Psalm 104:33–34

With Thanksgiving

Enable me, O God,
    to rejoice in thee always;
    to be careful for nothing;
    but in everything
    by prayer and supplication
    with thanksgiving,
    to make known my requests
    unto thee.
          —Philippians 4:4–6

Thou Crownest the Year

O God, thou art the confidence
    of all the ends of the earth,
    and of them that are afar off
    upon the sea.
Thou visitest the earth,
    and waterest it;
    thou greatly enrichest it
    with thy river which is full of water;
    thou preparest them corn,
    when thou hast so provided for it.
Thou waterest the ridges thereof
    abundantly;
    thou settlest the furrows thereof;
    thou makest it soft with showers;
    thou blessest the springing thereof.
Thou crownest the year
    with thy goodness;
    and the little hills rejoice
    on every side.
The pastures are clothed with flocks;
    the valleys also are covered with corn;
    they shout for joy; they also sing.
        —Psalm 65:5–13

More Than Conquerors

If thou, God, be for us
    who can be against us?

Thou, who spared not thine own Son
but delivered him up for us all,
how shalt thou not with him
also freely give us all things?
Who shall separate us
from thy love in Christ?
Shall tribulation, or distress,
or persecution, or famine,
or nakedness, or peril, or sword?
Nay, in all these things
we are more than conquerors
through thy love,
which is in Christ Jesus, our Lord.
—Romans 8:31–37

For All the Saints

We praise thee, O God,
and give heartfelt thanks
for all thy faithful
prophets and saints
who through faith
subdued kingdoms,
wrought righteousness,
stopped the mouths of lions,
quenched the violence of fire;
escaped the edge of the sword;
out of weakness were made strong;
were tortured,
not accepting deliverance;
had trial of cruel mockings
and scourgings;

were stoned, and slain with the sword;
wandered about in sheepskins
and goatskins, being destitute,
afflicted, tormented.
Wherefore, O God,
seeing that we also are compassed about
with so great a cloud of witnesses,
grant us grace to lay aside
every weight, and the sin
that doth so easily beset us,
and to run with patience
the race that is set before us,
looking unto Jesus,
the author and finisher of our faith,
who for the joy that was set before him,
endured the cross, despising the shame,
and is set down at the right hand
of thy throne, O God.
—Hebrews 11:33–37;12:1–2

The Depths of the Riches

O the depths of the riches
both of the wisdom
and knowledge
of thee, O God!
How unsearchable are thy judgments,
and thy ways are past finding out!
For of thee, and through thee,
and to thee are all things:
to whom be glory for ever.
—Romans 11:33–36

Gladness

Thou hast put gladness
in my heart, O Lord.
—Psalm 4:7

This Day

This is the day which thou hast made,
I will rejoice and be glad in it.
—Psalm 118:24

Ear and Eye

The hearing ear and the seeing eye,
thou, Lord, hast made
even both of them.
—Proverbs 20:12

Thy Greatness

O Lord my God, thou art very great;
thou art clothed with honour and majesty;
who coverest thyself with light
as with a garment;
who stretchest out the heavens
like a curtain;
who makest the clouds thy chariot;
who walkest upon the wings of the wind.

Thou sendest the springs into the valleys,
   which run among the hills.
     They give drink to every beast of the field.
     By them shall the fowls of the heaven
     have their habitation,
     which sing among the branches.
Thou causest the grass to grow for the cattle,
   and herb for the service of man;
     that he may bring forth food
     out of the earth.
Thy trees, Lord, are full of sap,
   the cedars of Lebanon which thou hast planted;
     where the birds make their nests;
     as for the stork, the fir trees are her house.
     The high hills are a refuge for the wild goats;
     and the rocks for the conies.
O Lord, how manifold are thy works!
   in wisdom hast thou made them all;
     the earth is full of thy riches.
          —Psalm 104 (selected verses)

Thou Heardest My Cry

I waited patiently for thee, O God;
   and thou didst incline unto me,
   and heardest my cry.
     Thou hast put a new song in my mouth,
     even praise unto thee, our God.
Many, O Lord my God,
   are thy wonderful works
   which thou hast done,
     and thy thoughts which are to us-ward.

Withhold not thou thy tender mercies
    from me, O Lord;
    let thy lovingkindness and thy truth
    continually preserve me.
    Let all those who seek thee
    rejoice and be glad in thee;
    let such as love thy salvation
    say continually,
    The Lord be magnified.
Thou art my help and my deliverance;
    make no tarrying, O my God.
                —Psalm 40 (selected verses)

We Are Glad

Thou, O Lord,
    hast done great things for us;
    whereof we are glad.
                —Psalm 126:3

Before I Was Afflicted

Thou hast dealt well with me, O Lord,
    according to thy word.
    Before I was afflicted,
    I went astray;
    but now I have kept thy word.
It is good for me
    that I have been afflicted,
    that I might learn thy statutes.

The law of thy mouth
   is better unto me than thousands
   of gold and silver.
I know, O Lord,
   that thy judgments are right,
   and that thou in faithfulness
   hast afflicted me.
Let, I pray thee,
   thy merciful kindness
   be for my comfort,
   according to thy word unto me.
          —Psalm 119:65–76

A *Lamp and a Light*

Thy word, O God,
   is a lamp unto my feet,
   and a light unto my path.
          —Psalm 119:105

Thy Mercy Endureth for Ever

I give thanks unto thee, O Lord;
   for thou art good;
   for thy mercy endureth for ever.
I give thanks unto thee, O Lord,
   to thee who alone doest great wonders;
   for thy mercy endureth for ever.
To thee who by wisdom made the heavens;
   for thy mercy endureth for ever.

To thee who stretched out the earth
   above the waters;
     for thy mercy endureth for ever.
To thee who made great lights;
     for thy mercy endureth for ever;
   the sun to rule by day;
     for thy mercy endureth for ever;
   the moon and stars to rule by night;
     for thy mercy endureth for ever.
I give thanks unto thee,
   God of heaven,
     for thy mercy endureth for ever.
          —Psalm 136:1–9,26

Happy Is He That Hath Thee

I praise thee, O Lord,
While I live, will I praise thee.
   I will sing praises to thee,
   O Lord, while I have any being.
Happy is he that hath thee,
   O God, for his help;
   whose hope is in thee, our God
   who made heaven, and earth, and sea,
   and all that is therein;
   who keepeth truth for ever;
   who executeth judgment
   for the oppressed;
   who giveth food to the hungry.
Thou, O God,
   dost loose the prisoners;
   thou dost open the eyes of the blind;

thou raisest them that are bowed down;
thou lovest the righteous;
thou preservest the stranger;
thou relievest the fatherless
and the widow;
but the way of the wicked
thou turnest upside down.
Thou, O Lord our God,
shalt reign for ever
unto all generations.
—Psalm 146:1–2,5–10

Praise Is Comely

We praise thee, O God;
for it is good to sing praises
unto thee, our God;
for it is pleasant
and praise is comely.
Thou, Lord, dost heal
the broken in heart
and bind up their wounds.
Thou tellest the number of the stars;
thou callest them all by their names.
Great art thou, our God,
and of great power;
thine understanding is infinite.
We sing unto thee, O Lord,
with thanksgiving.
—Psalm 147:1–7

Thy Lovingkindnesses

I will mention thy lovingkindnesses
 O God, according to all
 that thou hast bestowed upon me,
 and thy great goodness toward thy people,
 which thou hast bestowed upon us
 according to thy mercies
 and the multitude
 of thy lovingkindnesses.
                    —Isaiah 63:7

Rejoice and Be Exceeding Glad

Grant us grace, O God,
 to rejoice and be exceeding glad
 when men revile us,
 and persecute us,
 and say all manner of evil
 against us, falsely,
 for thy sake;
 knowing that great is our reward
 in heaven, for so persecuted they
 the prophets that were before us.
                    —Matthew 5:11–12

We Praise Thee

Thou, O God,
 dost cover the heavens with clouds,
 thou preparest rain for the earth,
 and makest grass to grow
 upon the mountains.
 Thou givest to the beast his food,
 and to the young ravens which cry.
Thou delightest not
 in the strength of the horse;
 thou takest no pleasure
 in the legs of a man.
 Thou takest pleasure in them that fear thee,
 in those that hope in thy mercy.
We praise thee, O God.
   —Psalm 147:8–12

Thanks for All Things

May we be filled with the Spirit,
 speaking to each other
 in psalms and hymns
 and spiritual songs,
 singing and making melody
 in our hearts to thee, O Lord;
 giving thanks always
 for all things unto thee,
 O Lord, in the name of our Lord
Jesus Christ.
   —Ephesians 5:18–20

Glory in Tribulation

Being justified by faith, O God,
   we have peace with thee,
   through our Lord, Jesus Christ,
   by whom also
   we have access by faith
   into this grace wherein we stand,
   and rejoice in the hope of thy glory,
   O God. And not only so,
   but we glory in tribulation also
   knowing that tribulation
   worketh patience,
   and patience, experience,
   and experience, hope.
And hope maketh not ashamed
   because thy love, O God,
   is shed abroad in our hearts
   by the Holy Spirit
   which is given unto us.
          —Romans 5:1–5

Thy Holy Spirit

We rejoice, O God,
   that as many of us
   as are led by thy Spirit,
   we are thy sons.
   For we have not received
   the spirit of bondage to fear;

but we have received
the Spirit of adoption,
whereby we cry, Abba, Father.
The Spirit itself beareth witness
with our spirit
that we are thy children, O God.
And if children, then heirs;
heirs of thine, O God,
and joint heirs with Christ;
if so be that we suffer with him,
that we may be also
glorified together.
For we believe that the sufferings
of this present time
are not worthy to be compared
with the glory
that shall be revealed in us.
And we know that all things
work together for good
to them that love thee, O God,
to them that are called
according to thy purpose.
—Romans 8:14–18,28

Yet Will I Rejoice

Although the fig tree shall not blossom,
neither shall fruit be in the vines;
the labour of the olive shall fail,
and the fields shall yield no meat,
the flock shall be cut off from the fold,
and there shall be no herd in the stalls:

Yet will I rejoice in thee,
   O Lord, I will joy in thee,
   O God of my salvation.
               —Habakkuk 3:17–18

The Shepherd Psalm

Thou art my shepherd, Lord;
   I shall not want.
   Thou makest me to lie down
   in green pastures;
   thou leadest me beside the still waters.
   Thou restorest my soul;
   thou leadest me in the paths
   of righteousness for thy name's sake.
Yea, though I walk through the valley
   of the shadow of death,
   I will fear no evil:
   for thou art with me;
   thy rod and thy staff they comfort me.
Thou preparest a table before me
   in the presence of mine enemies;
   thou anointest my head with oil;
   my cup runneth over.
Surely goodness and mercy
   shall follow me
   all the days of my life;
   and I will dwell in thy house
   O Lord, for ever.
               —Psalm 23

Nothing Can Separate Us from Thy Love

Father, we rejoice
    that neither death, nor life,
    nor angels, nor principalities,
    nor powers, nor things present,
    nor things to come,
    nor height, nor depth,
    nor any other creature,
    shall be able to separate us
    from thy love, O God,
    which is in Christ Jesus, our Lord.
           —Romans 8:38–39

A Goodly Heritage

Preserve me, O God,
    for in thee do I put my trust.
    Thou, Lord, art the portion
    of mine inheritance and of my cup;
    thou maintainest my lot.
    The lines are fallen for me
    in pleasant places,
    yea, I have a goodly heritage.
I will bless thee, O Lord, my heart is glad.
    Thou wilt show me the path of life:
    In thy presence is fulness of joy.
    At thy right hand there are
    pleasures for evermore.
           —Psalm 16:1,5–11

Daily Benefits

Blessed be thou, O Lord,
　who daily loadest us
　with benefits.
　　　　　—Psalm 68:19

Patience

Grant, O God,
　that we may count it all joy
　when we fall into divers temptations,
　knowing this,
　that the trying of our faith
　worketh patience,
　and letting patience
　have her perfect work,
　that we may be perfect and entire.
　　　　　—James 1:2–4

Giving Thanks for All Things

Give us grace
　to walk as children of light;
　giving thanks always for all things
　unto thee, God our Father,
　in the name of our Lord, Jesus Christ.
　　　　　—Ephesians 5:8,20

Make Us Glad

Make us glad, O God,
 according to the days
 wherein thou hast afflicted us,
 and the days wherein
 we have seen evil.
    —Psalm 90:15

All That Is Within Me

My soul shall bless thee, O Lord,
 my soul and all that is within me
 shall bless thy holy name.
My soul shall bless thee,
 and shall not forget all thy benefits;
 who forgivest all mine iniquities;
 who healest all my diseases;
 who redeemest my life
 from destruction;
 who crownest me with lovingkindness
 and tender mercies.
    —Psalm 103:1–4

With My Whole Heart

I will praise thee, O Lord,
 with my whole heart;
 I will show forth
 all thy marvelous works;

I will be glad
and rejoice in thee;
I will sing praises
to thy name,
O thou most High.
            —Psalm 9:1–2

Thou Hast Dealt Bountifully

I have trusted in thy mercy;
    my heart shall rejoice
    in thy salvation.
I will sing unto thee, O Lord,
    because thou hast
    dealt bountifully with me.
            —Psalm 13:5–6

With Joyfulness Giving Thanks

We give thanks unto thee, O God,
    the Father of our Lord Jesus Christ.
    We pray that we may be filled
    with the knowledge of thy will
    in all wisdom
    and spiritual understanding;
    that we may walk worthy of thee, O God,
    being fruitful in every good work,
    and increasing in the knowledge of thee;
    strengthened with all might,
    according to thy glorious power,
    unto all patience and longsuffering,

with joyfulness giving thanks
unto thee, our Father,
who hast made us meet to be
partakers of the inheritance
of the saints in light;
who hast delivered us
from the power of darkness
and hast translated us
into the kingdom of thy dear Son.
　　　　—Colossians 1:3,9–13

Let the Earth Rejoice

Thou, O Lord, reignest;
　let the earth rejoice;
　let the multitude of isles
　be glad thereof.
　Clouds and darkness
　are round about thee;
　righteousness and judgment
　are the habitation of thy throne.
Thy lightnings enlightened the world;
　the earth saw and trembled.
　The hills melted like wax
　at thy presence, O Lord,
　at thy presence, O Lord of the whole earth.
The heavens declare thy righteousness,
　and all the people see thy glory.
　For thou, O Lord,
　art high above all the earth.
Light is sown for the righteous,
　and gladness

for the upright in heart.
We rejoice in thee, O Lord;
and give thanks
at the remembrance of thy holiness.
—Psalm 97 (selected verses)

In the Night Watches

O God, thou art my God;
    my mouth shall praise thee
    with joyful lips,
    when I remember thee upon my bed,
    and meditate on thee
    in the night watches.
Because thou hast been my help,
    therefore in the shadow of thy wings
    will I rejoice.
    My soul followeth hard after thee;
    thy right hand upholdeth me.
        —Psalm 63:1–8

Rejoice Evermore

Grant me grace, O God,
    to rejoice evermore;
    in everything
    to give thanks,
    knowing that this
    is thy will for me.
        —I Thessalonians 5:16,18

Thy Grace Is Sufficient

Grant us faith to know
   that thy grace
   is sufficient for us,
   for thy strength
   is made perfect in weakness.
Help us most gladly
   to glory in our infirmities
   that the power of Christ
   may rest upon us.
                    —II Corinthians 12:9

Whether We Live or Die

We thank thee, O God,
   that whether we live,
   we live unto thee,
   or whether we die,
   we die unto thee;
   whether we live, therefore,
   or die, we are thine.
                    —Romans 14:8

Thou Wilt Light My Candle

I will love thee, O Lord my strength.
   Thou art my rock and my fortress,
   and my deliverer, my God,

my strength, in whom I will trust.
Thou wilt light my candle,
O Lord my God,
and enlighten my darkness.
Therefore will I give thanks
unto thee, O God,
and sing praises to thy name.
—Psalm 18:1–2,28,49

New Every Morning

Thy mercies and compassions
fail not, O Lord.
They are new every morning;
great is thy faithfulness.
Thou art my portion;
therefore will I hope in thee.
Thou art good
unto them that wait for thee,
to the soul that seeketh thee.
—Lamentations 3:22–25

Let the Nations Be Glad

God, be merciful unto us, and bless us;
and cause thy face to shine upon us;
that thy way may be known upon earth,
thy saving health among all nations.
Let the people praise thee, O God;
let all the people praise thee.
O let the nations be glad
and sing for joy;

for thou shalt judge the people
righteously, and govern
the nations upon earth.
Let the people praise thee, O God;
let all the people praise thee.
Then shall the earth
yield her increase,
and thou, our own God,
shalt bless us.
Thou shalt bless us,
and all the ends of the earth
shall fear thee.
—Psalm 67

Girded with Gladness

I will extol thee, O Lord,
for thou hast lifted me up.
O Lord my God, I cried unto thee
and thou hast healed me.
I give thanks
at the remembrance of thy holiness.
Weeping may endure for a night,
but joy cometh in the morning.
Thou hast turned for me
my mourning into dancing;
thou hast put off my sackcloth
and girded me with gladness.
O Lord my God,
I will give thanks unto thee
for ever.
—Psalm 30:1–5,11–12

Amen and Amen

Blessed be thou, Lord God,
  from everlasting to everlasting.
Amen and Amen.
      —Psalm 41:13

In Conclusion

The book is finished. And it is the compiler's prayer that each reader may find in its use: a new awareness of God's reality and omnipresence; a more vivid companionship with Jesus, God's Word to us today as to those of earlier generations; and a deepening experience of the indwelling presence of the Holy Spirit, enriching and guiding each moment of life.

Father, thou hast said:

> As the rain cometh down,
> and the snow from heaven,
> and returneth not thither,
> but watereth the earth,
> and maketh it bring forth and bud,
> that it may give seed to the sower,
> and bread to the eater;
> so shall my word be
> that goeth forth out of my mouth:
> it shall not return unto me void,
> but it shall accomplish
> that which I please,
> and it shall prosper
> in the thing whereto I sent it.
> —Isaiah 55:10–11

So be it, Holy Father. Alleluia, Amen!

Index

I. SELECTED BIBLICAL PROMISES

II. SELECTED BIBLICAL PRAYERS